Stitch with Style

BEVERLY RUSH

Madrona Publishers, Inc.   *Seattle*

Connecting Threads

STITCH WITH STYLE

WEAVE WITH STYLE

KNIT WITH STYLE

ALSO BY BEVERLY RUSH:

The Stitchery Idea Book, Van Nostrand Reinhold, 1974

Library of Congress Cataloging in Publication Data

Rush, Beverly 1930–
  Stitch with style.

  (Connecting threads)
  1. Needlework.   2. Embroidery.   I. Title.
II. Series
TT715.R87   746.4′4   79-14559
ISBN 0-914842-39-0 pbk.

Acknowledgments

  This book is totally dependent on the artists whose names appear throughout the pages with the work. My thanks to them all. Those close enough to have given constant support and encouragement have made my life richer: Jacqueline Enthoven, Jill Nordfors, Mary Ann Spawn. Others I have counted on repeatedly have been Bruce Bleckert, Mary Watson, Joise Jewitt, and the editorial staff of Madrona Publishers.

Madrona Publishers, Inc.
2116 Western Avenue
Seattle, Washington 98121

Drawings by Jill Nordfors
Supplementary drawings by Beth Workman
All photos by the author unless otherwise noted

Contents

WHERE TO START   3

PLANNING   4

ANALYZING THE GARMENT   6

MATERIALS   8

DESIGN   10
Adapting, 15; Abstracting, 22;
Enlarging or Reducing, 24

MARKING METHODS   26
Transfer Methods, 26; Templates, 27;
Nylon Net, 27; Waste Canvas, 27;
Basting Threads, 27; Marking Tools, 28

MAKING THE GARMENT   29

TECHNIQUES   31
Appliqué, 31; The Small Touch, 40;
Vests, 43; Surface Stitchery, 48

SPECIAL FABRICS 75

Patterned Fabrics (Print or Woven), 75;
Metallics, 78; Other Fabrics, 81;
Ultrasuede, 81

FINISHING TOUCHES 85

GLOSSARY OF STITCHES 89

STYLE SHOW (color section)

Follows page 28

Facing Page

(Top) *Ensemble of charcoal wool yarns—light and dark—woven, knitted, and embroidered: a collaboration of the three authors of this series. Skirt and sleeves by Jean Wilson, author of* Weave with Style, *her newest of seven books on weaving; embellishment, in gray and rust novelty yarns, by this author; and knitted coat body of twisted stockinette stitch, knit by Jane Thompson and designed by Ferne Cone, author of* Knit with Style, *her newest of three books on knitting.*

(Bottom) *Detail of stitched yoke and shoulder area. Gray, curly novelty yarn couched with overlying lines of single strands of wool held in place with stem stitches also worked over as a return couching.*

Never has a time been more exciting for embroidery for clothing. After the casualness of the sixties and early seventies, the fashion world is once again featuring elegant clothing. Designers have reinstated real silks, fine woolens, crisp cottons, and linens. (These natural fibers never disappeared from top designer lines.) Even when synthetics are used, they are likely to be made and named in imitation of the desired "real thing." And, perhaps inspired by disco fever, perhaps just following the normal reverse swing of the pendulum of taste, people are again dressing up.

Along with this renewed appreciation of elegance and natural fibers has remained a healthy appreciation of individual style and a respect for the handmade. The growth of needle skills in this country (and others) has resulted in a number of people able to create handmade embroidery of exquisite beauty. Some of their embroidery has become an important feature of well-designed clothing. In an age of mechanization, the beauty created by the talent and hand of an artist has become rarer than ever, and in the marketplace, rarity can become a valued asset.

Already contemporary handmade clothing is appearing and being sold in art galleries. Leading fashion designers are featuring more embroidery on their apparel. Collections for 1978 by St. Laurent, Givenchy, and Karl Lagerfeld, for Chloe, all show heavily bead-embellished jackets and dresses. Jean-Louis Scherrer has been quoted in *W* (Fairchild Publications) as saying that he paid $500 for a sample of handmade embroidery, of which there are dozens hanging around his atelier. Of his eighty-piece collection, at least

Beige, handloomed fabric from India embellished with Teneriffe wheels, silk tassels, and needle lace. By Helen Richards.

twenty-three items will be hand-embroidered. This designer says, "... embroidery is pure art. The day one makes embroidery on a machine, it's not haute couture."

While not everyone creates pure art, many stitchers are very skillful in working a design. What remains is to add to this technical skill the ideas, taste, and design sense to use the craft to its best advantage. This book is a start in that direction. I hope it will be a tool which enables you to begin a continuing exploration of how you can best use your embroidery to enhance the beauty of your finest clothing.

2

Where to Start

Sliced shells highlight rows of free stitching by Helen Richards. Of handloomed fabric from India, the garment has traveled throughout the world and is easily washed in hotel bathtubs.

The ability to do embroidery has grown faster than the ability to plan embroidery. Clothing embroidery sounds like an easy thing to plan. A nice little touch can be easily added to many garments, but to make stitchery an integral part of a coordinated, overall plan or design does not just happen.

Helen Richards, a well-known fiber artist, is among those who have recently renewed an interest in clothing design. She sees her return, after twenty-five years, as a "... quiet rebellion against all the ethnic garments purchased around the world that just didn't seem to come off when someone else wore them besides the original owner.... the inspirational construction and embellishments are so beautiful, but they didn't fit me, or function in my life style." This started her looking for beautiful fabrics and thread to use in a new way. She also did a great deal of research in costume collections of museums, looking at clothing of the mid-Victorian era and later. "... these are my heritage. The beautiful cutwork and white embroidery on summer afternoon dresses. The braids (which sent me back to tatting, but with heavier threads) the ruching (narrow ruffles or pleated strips of cloth or lace) and the beading on wintertime wools. Why couldn't my clothing be that individual?"

3

Contemporary dress from Mexico. A blue cotton/poly fabric of medium weave shows off the brightly colored animals of cotton floss.

Planning

The planning stage presents an obstacle to many, and to help people overcome this obstacle is a major purpose of this book.

In general, there seem to be two approaches to planning the embroidered area of a garment. One person will select certain lines or areas to work within, possibly making a few guide marks for perimeter or placement, then work freely within that area. This is most successful when the number of stitches, the color range, or the shapes are closely related and limited. Helen Richards says she has "a tendency to over-embellish, but feel I can get away with it because of a limited color palette." Notice the affinity to each other of Mary Ann Spawn's mosaic of stitches, worked very freely, but with an artist's sensitivity to color and texture.

The other approach to planning embroidery is to work out the total design very carefully on paper, then to transfer the drawn lines to the material for careful execution. Both methods have their advantages, and many stitchers will use both, choosing whichever is best suited to a particular design or technique.

To plan you need to draw. So many have a built-in fear of drawing: you were told as a child that you were not an artist, therefore, don't try to draw. Yet any fingers that can manipulate a needle can also draw. Stitchers have an advantage because their finger muscles are in better shape than those that have not been used for small manipulations. A large part of learning to draw is training these very muscles to move your tool (pen *or* needle) to where you want it to go. The other part of drawing is training the eye—teaching it to really see lines and shapes, to separate these from the confusion of the world around them so that you can repeat them on your paper.

Even doodling can result in pleasing shapes. Learn to see lines and shapes that intrigue you and practice putting them on paper. Most of us, today, do not have beautiful handwriting, yet we do not hesitate to jot off a note or a letter for another to read. Sketching should be viewed as simply a form of jotting down a note, and it need be meant for only you to "read." As long as it reminds you of the good visual idea that prompted it, it is sufficient. Anyone can sketch on this level. With practice, anyone with the finger coordination of a stitcher can also learn to refine this sketch and produce pleasing, if simple, working drawings.

Another aid to becoming comfortable when working with a drawing pad is a visit to an art store. There are innumerable graphic tools used by professionals for the very reason that they simplify drawing. Templates can be bought in various shapes and sizes. French curves make graceful lines to build on. See-through rulers or T squares make lining up rows easy. None of these things is expensive or takes special learning to use: we'll be referring to them in our planning. The ability to draw can be improved as easily as you can, or did, improve your ability with the needle. Neither happens overnight, and in each you start with the simplest steps. And while we are not out to make a drawing artist of you, you'll soon find that with even a moderate amount of practice, whole new design possibilities are open to you.

Inexpensive tools from an art store can make designing easy for even a nonartist.

Analyzing the Garment

It's not simply a matter of arranging lines on paper, of course. In planning embroidery for clothing, you must also consider the garment.

Look for seam lines, silhouettes, and styles that support the style and techniques you want to work in. If in doubt, choose a garment of simple lines and few seams. When the pattern is constructed with prominent seams, make sure they reinforce your design ideas by providing a good working space or working lines.

Trace your garment pattern over the illustrated garment which is closest in outside shape, or silhouette, to yours. Sketch in your particular neckline, sleeve shape, and any

6

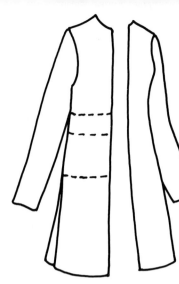

garment shape for each, then varying the placement or scale of whatever embroidery you would like to do. Would something work better with a modification of the garment pattern itself: would fuller sleeves or a different neckline be better? Work at this until you know the area you want to fill and the relative size of the motif you want.

At this point you are ready to determine what stitching technique you will use. Even if you have had something in mind from the very first, you may find yourself changing your mind as you explore possibilities on paper. Scale, among other things, can be a determining factor. If your sketches lead you to want the entire yoke resplendent in stitches that continue down the bodice, you may well think twice before planning to do tiny intricate stitches and choose instead something which will work up more quickly.

7

A variety of fabrics—Thai silks, metallics, prints— appliquéd on the lower part of a vest of brushed velvet. The overlying grid of stitched lines creates a strong unity (full vest seen on first page of color section and on page 80). By Mary Ann Spawn.

Materials

Most of us select materials because they are visually pleasing. Today's fibers are too diverse to categorize neatly, so it is important, when choosing materials, to develop the habit of carefully reading labels, especially noting the fiber content and care instructions.

When a combination of fibers is to be used on one garment, plan to care for the whole according to the needs of the most fragile fiber involved. It is worth the time spent to test washing methods beforehand. This includes washing together all the fibers you plan to use, since some colors will bleed into one fiber but not another. For instance, we probably have all had the experience of only one thing in a load of wash taking on the color of something else in the load, while others remain unchanged. When in doubt about the washability of anything, it is best to have it dry-cleaned.

Special fibers and materials and some of their characteristics are discussed later in the book. Your selection of both fabrics and threads should be carefully planned to suit your technique. A beautiful idea that presents monumental obstacles to working or matching might not be the happiest choice.

8

(Top) *Stitch detail on velour top. The freely worked bullion and stem stitches of cotton perle go well with both the texture and stretchiness of the cotton velour (full neckline on page 72). By Mary Ann Spawn.*

(Center) *Appliqué of Ultrasuede on the back of a jeans jacket by Melinda Phillips. The washable synthetic suede is blind-stitched in patterns similar to Yugoslavian embroidery.*

(Bottom) *Concord's Kettle Cloth, a popular cotton/poly weave to use for stitchery, embellished with perle cottons and shi sha mirrors. By Mary Ann Spawn.*

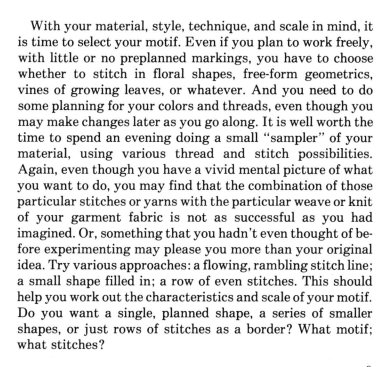

With your material, style, technique, and scale in mind, it is time to select your motif. Even if you plan to work freely, with little or no preplanned markings, you have to choose whether to stitch in floral shapes, free-form geometrics, vines of growing leaves, or whatever. And you need to do some planning for your colors and threads, even though you may make changes later as you go along. It is well worth the time to spend an evening doing a small "sampler" of your material, using various thread and stitch possibilities. Again, even though you have a vivid mental picture of what you want to do, you may find that the combination of those particular stitches or yarns with the particular weave or knit of your garment fabric is not as successful as you had imagined. Or, something that you hadn't even thought of before experimenting may please you more than your original idea. Try various approaches: a flowing, rambling stitch line; a small shape filled in; a row of even stitches. This should help you work out the characteristics and scale of your motif. Do you want a single, planned shape, a series of smaller shapes, or just rows of stitches as a border? What motif; what stitches?

9

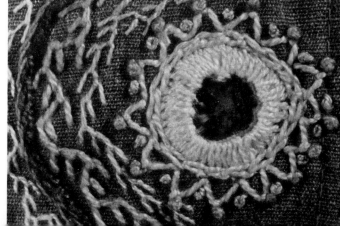

A decorative frieze on a garden fountain provides motifs adapted and rearranged for embroidery on a wool knit. The stitches go through both pattern-traced webbing and fabric. After the stitches are complete, the webbing is torn away.

Design

Notes from Jack Lenor Larsen's graduate class on fabric design at the University of Washington include his formula: (motif x scale x material x technique x use = design.) It is *design* that is the total of all of these ingredients. The quality of each and the harmony of the combination of these elements influences that total.

Unless you enjoy embroidery just for the sake of busy hands (which is, after all, a valid reason), it is worth your time to study design. The more you expose yourself to good design and design ideas, the easier your own job of designing will become. But because you will collect many and diverse ideas, you will probably want to record, organize, and store them as you acquire them. This will help you find them later when you need them for your own work. When collecting data, it helps to develop a filing system. Noting each subject or idea, when you discover it, on an index card or separate sheet of small notepaper will make it easy to file each card or sheet under its own category later.

Study the embroidery and textiles of other cultures and other eras. Learn what influences were at work on the artists, what fibers and dyes were available in a particular area, what forms and shapes their designs took, what symbolism was used, what techniques were employed, what tools were available. Look for related design motifs in other media of the same time and culture: architecture, paintings, prints, metal and wood crafts. Who did the work: slaves or household help? the women or the men of the family? individual artisans or guilds? Find out if embroidery was available to

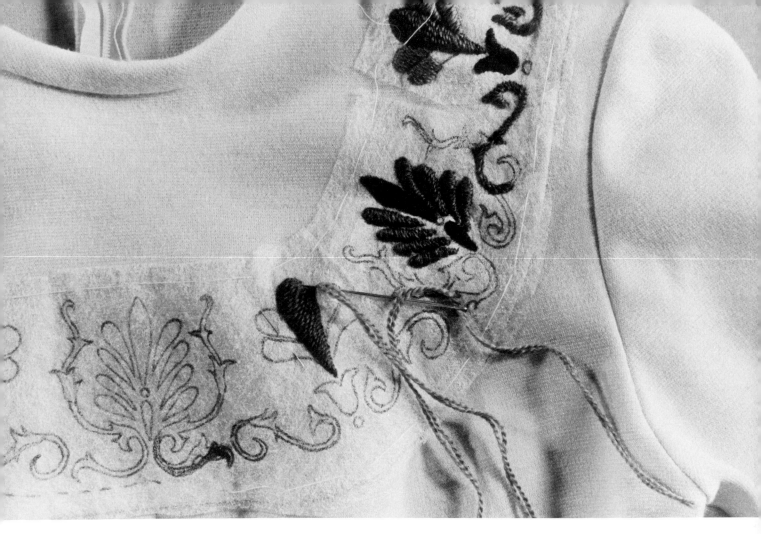

everyone. Often only the wealthy or the royal could afford ornate work, with simpler techniques and fibers used by and for the peasants. Embroidery can make the people of another time and another place seem alive.

Travel provides exciting opportunities for studying embroidery. Learn ahead of time which museums in the area you will be visiting have embroidery collections. A letter sent ahead may make special studies or viewing possible. Read up on what is typical of the area. The more you know before you go, the more you will know what to look for and what to ask. If embroidery is still being made, learn where it

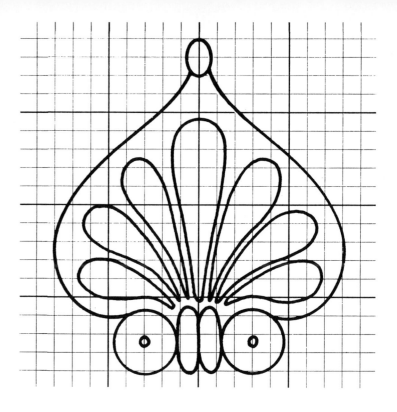

Design motif taken from a gold artifact of Pompeii to complement the "Roman-coin" button. The side seam of the finished tie is slit, to allow the embroidery to be added to the finished garment, and will be closed with blind stitches.

Empty slide mounts to be filled for design exploration.

can be seen or bought. Look into local markets, stalls, or small shops, as well as the better-known galleries. (I also like to see what needlework and fabric supplies, or books, can be bought in other areas—in this country as well as others. Ideas abound, some different than anything I have seen at home.)

Study the quality of the materials and of the stitching as well as the traditional patterns and materials. Work often varies from village to village. In general, few artists are known by name. Most craftwork, especially in fibers, is done anonymously. Not many people are very knowledgeable about the textiles of their country. Don't be discouraged from asking. And continue to ask important questions, even after you feel you have gotten the answer. You may pick up a different point of view, additional information, or enough to know the first answer was wrong.

Take a magnifying glass, and use it often. The museums and better shops and galleries will be good places to learn something of standards of quality before you do any buying.

Since a camera is a convenient tool, most of us will use one, at least on travels. But general travel snapshots are of little value. You must deliberately look for and record design and motif ideas. After every trip I pull out all those photos taken especially for design ideas and file them separately. They may be of nature, sculpture, ironwork, carved stone, or other decor on buildings: a beautiful hinge on a door; a pattern in a carpet; tiles underfoot. Every place in life offers design possibilities, once the eye is trained to see them. Then the camera can be used as a sketchpad—to catch the lines and shapes that intrigued you, not to produce well-balanced photos per se. Like your sketches, these photos are not meant to be showpieces but are usable reminders, to you, of design ideas.

An interesting approach to using a slide projector for design ideas is to make your own slides by inserting a variety of materials into an empty slide mount. Several types of mounts are available: cardboard, plastic, aluminum. You may have to go to a fairly big photo supply store to find them (or order by mail from one of the bigger houses advertised in photo magazines). Some come with thin sheets of glass meant for protecting the slides. For others you will have to cut clear acrylic (bought at art supply stores) to fit where the slide film should go. The ones I use have two thin sheets of glass and snap shut. Anything thin enough and cut to size will fit between them. These can be reopened and used repeatedly.

Needless to say, working "slide size" means working small—either slightly smaller than 1-by-1 1/2 inches or approximately 1 1/2 inches square, according to format. Using an empty frame as a viewfinder will help you locate a surprising number of things to try in it. Designs on gift-wrap paper show up well because of the plain back. A magazine print may or may not work, depending on what is printed on the back. The same is true of fabric prints. The amount of light coming through the material can make the woven threads overshadow anything printed on them. One of my favorite slide materials is tiny snippets of yarn and thread,

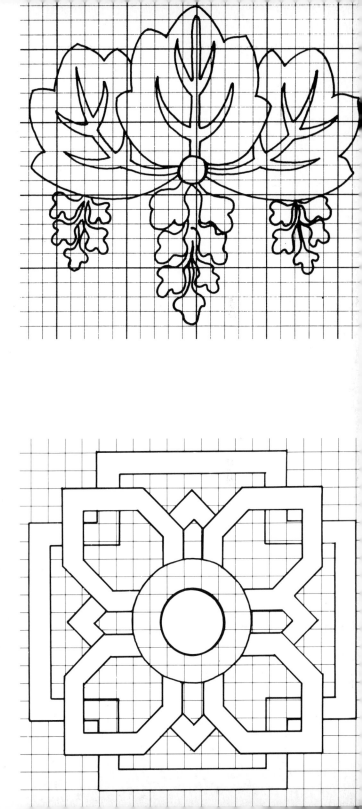

Detail of silk embroidery on Japanese obi. From the collection of Jean Wilson.

Silk butterfly on Chinese panel. Courtesy of Carole Fiege.

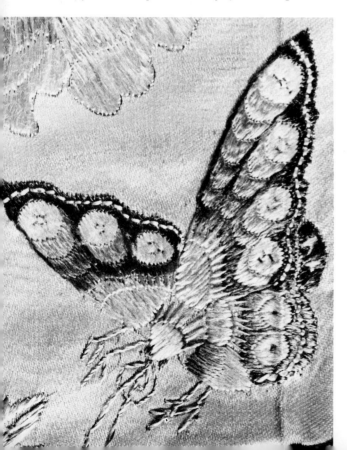

including metallics. To see them enlarged on the screen with strong light behind them is most interesting.

You can insert small sketches or tracings on paper. You can draw shapes right on the glass, or on a clear piece of acrylic, with colored marking pens (permanent pens will mark glass or plastic; non-permanent ones work on paper). Cut pieces of colored tissue paper or cellophane can be used. Artist Janet Kummerlein uses small cuts of colored theatrical gel (a plastic film used to cover stage lights) and rubber cement to make slides with her classes. The rubber cement bubbles slightly with the heat of the projector lamp, adding texture to the image. In general, you must look for things that will transmit enough light to carry the color with them and not set up a blocking shadow.

Again and again, the need is to train your eye to recognize and select what is pleasing to you. A graceful line or an intriguing shape can be as exciting by itself as the lines and shapes combined to form a leaf. We are all familiar and therefore comfortable with the shape of the paisley or the ogee, yet these are not recognizable as subjects in nature, although they may have been before they were abstracted to become their own shapes. They are both pleasing and graceful—similar to shapes and forms seen in nature, but not representative of any one thing.

Discovering the freedom and the absolutely inexhaustible supply of sources for creating your own motif with little or no help is an exhilarating experience, and I urge you to try it. The secret is in learning to *adapt*.

14

ADAPTING

Many people do not clearly understand the difference between *adapting* a design and *copying* a design. To copy another's idea exactly, or to use a pattern just as it comes, takes the least creative and emotional involvement on the part of the doer, although the amount of time and work spent stitching remains the same. Copies often miss because they are so mindless that they do not have any real identity, style, or taste.

Yet most top designers freely *adapt* ideas. They pull ideas and influences from many sources into their own work. But they combine and rework borrowed ideas, making their designs decidedly different from the originals, even though the influences may be recognized. To each design, the professional brings his experience. And he brings knowledge: of color; of fabric possibilities; of how a small part of a motif can be pulled out to become the dominant instead of the minor motif; of how a single motif can be pulled out of a complex design and used by itself or repeated in a new way. He might add several motifs together, taking one idea from a fabric of a certain era and combining it with an architectural motif of the same period. Or a motif that looks quite dated might be translated into current fashion colors, completely changing its effect. The more knowledge you bring to any design, the more strength and harmony it is likely to have.

An important key to adaptation is simplification, of which exaggeration is an example. By simplifying a motif, a large piece of work can be done in the same number of hours as it takes to do a small, intricate piece. Ruth Dayan speaks of the work of Maskit, a crafts organization founded by her in

(Top) *Traditional yoke showing couching known as Bethlehem embroidery.* (Bottom) *A contemporary exaggeration of the same type of work, with simpler design, heavier threads. Courtesy of Ruth Dayan.*

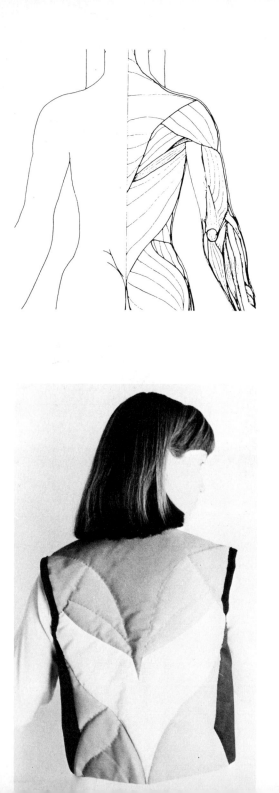

Robbie Fanning in a vest whose design was adapted from a drawing by husband, Tony, of surface muscles of a back. Margo Wing made the vest, then quilted it after Tony painted the muscle shapes in red, orange, black, and white Versatex. The two presented it to Robbie as a surprise. Photo and drawing by Tony Fanning.

Israel, which takes the best design ideas and techniques from the heritage of Israel's diverse immigrants and adapts them for use today. The making of objects based on these designs provides a source of income for today's craftworkers. One of Maskit's major design techniques is to *exaggerate*, taking single motifs from complex designs to use as the themes for new, simpler designs, which are then worked in larger stitches and thicker yarns. The motifs are greatly simplified, but the essence and the character of the originals are still there.

A single motif from a large, scrolled, intricate piece of Bethlehem couching is worked by itself, in heavier cording, couched to a band across the yoke of a dress. The band, contrasting in color to the stripe of the dress, sets off this single piece with all the beauty of old.

Another step in your design work is to refine an idea or a sketch—to get from that first quick, rough sketch to a finished guide for use with your garments. The easiest way for me is to work with several sheets of tracing paper, refining in successive repeats, each time emphasizing the lines that seem to be right, changing those that still need work. One by one, another line or area will seem to be okay, until the last tracing will be largely cleaning up the lines and refining the sketchy parts. When working with motifs of either two-way or four-way symmetry, I only refine one-half or one-quarter, respectively, of the design. The tracing paper is then folded in half and the lines retraced on the reverse side of the second half. (The lines will be clearly visible from both sides of the paper.) Four-way symmetry involves a second folding, from the opposite direction, and this time a retracing of both quarters that have already been marked.

16

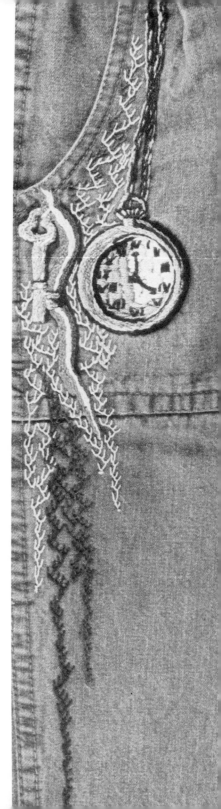

Trompe l'oeil, the painter's technique for super-realism, is a natural for stitchery. A watch and key dangle from a pocket, and sewing paraphernalia collect at the hem of jeans. By Mary Ann Spawn.

Red, handwoven linen jacket with Peruvian patterns, some stitched subtly in matching yarns, others highlighted by white. By Jean Wilson.

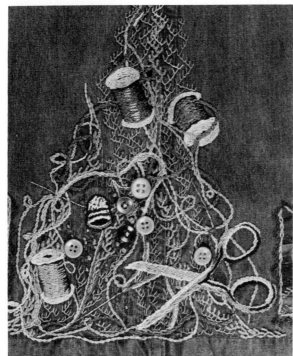

Akha woman's jacket, Burma. Handloomed cotton with back panel of appliqué and stitchery using market fabrics and threads.

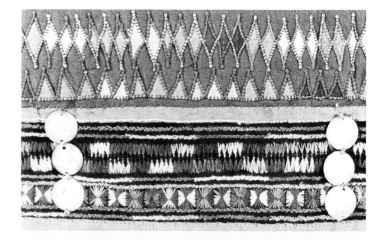

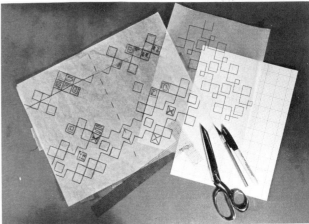

Design evolving from diamond repeats found on Akha jacket. A second tracing was used when cutting turquoise Ultrasuede with a ruler and X-acto knife. Yoke and waist seams of the dress's front panel were joined before being appliquéd. Stitchery was added to extend the design; then the dress was completed, as shown on third page of color section.

(Top right) Young Meo woman in northern Thailand village working on cross-stitch band to be later incorporated in a skirt. She works from the back of the black, handwoven cotton.

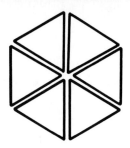
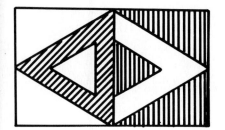
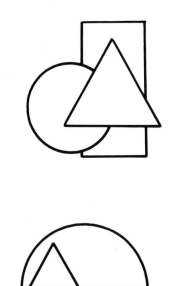

Adapting a motif

Once you have arrived at your final single motif, you can let it lead you on to a wealth of variations, repeats, and expansions. You can make it fit any area, emphasize it, or use it as a springboard to a more complex design. Using a simple equilateral triangle as an example motif, the following possibilities emerge:

1. The single motif.
2. Mirror images.
    - Side by side.
    - Up and down.
    - Four or more ways.
3. Counterchange.
4. Offset.
5. Grouped with related shapes to form a new single unit.
    - Random placement.
    - Overlapping.
6. Original shape within another shape, distorted to fit, if necessary.
7. Shapes within original shape.
    - Separate shapes formed by lines within motif.
    - Shapes formed by simple divisions of space, as with a triangle which has no interior lines.

So far, these exercises have used the single shape in what is still a single unit, but one of increased complexity. Any of

20

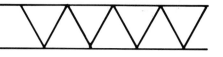

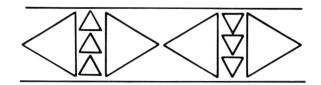

these units, as well as your original motif, may be used as repeated patterns.

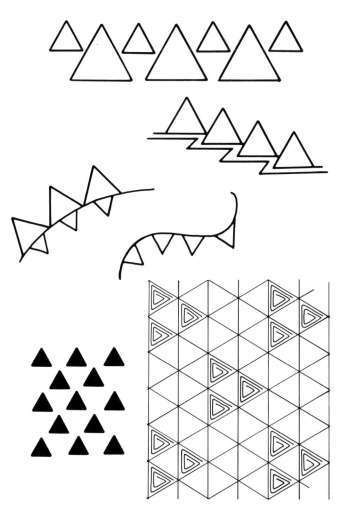

1. Line up in a single row for a border repeat.
    Alternate directions within the row.
    Alternate sizes within the row.
    Combine change of direction and change of sizes.
    Try this both with and without lines defining the band area.
    Try several rows together, in line or staggered.
2. Float clustered motifs or units at random in a larger space, keeping them fairly equal distances apart.
    Bring together in clusters throughout the space.
    Concentrate most of the clusters along the bottom line, still randomly.
    Increase the size of some of the clustered motifs.
3. Draw a curved line and repeat the motif along the curve.
4. Make a grid—straight lines, ogee, fish scale—any dividing lines that complement your motif. Place the motif within the grid in various ways: every other space; randomly; along one line; in one area, leaving others open.

21

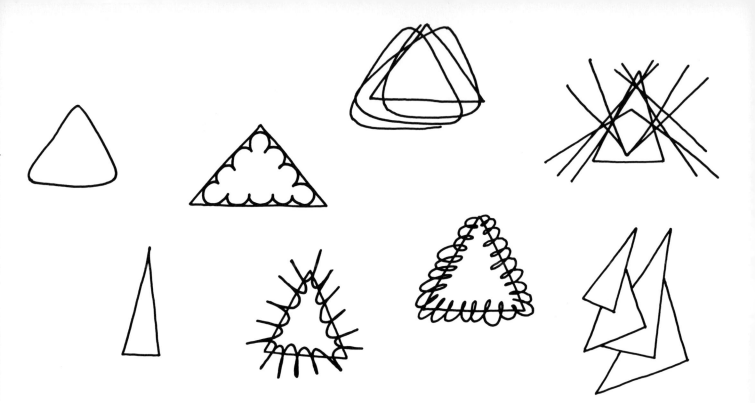

ABSTRACTING

So far our variations, while distorting the motif somewhat, have kept it generally intact. Following are some ideas to help you use your motif for abstracting—evolving entirely new shapes. Work quickly, using a broad-tip marking pen and a large tablet of paper. Unless suggested otherwise, each trial refers back to your original motif.

1. Draw a quick, freehand sketch of your motif.
2. Elongate it, sketching one taller and narrower than your first.
3. Squash it, sketching one shorter and fatter.
4. Look at your motif. Draw it as though it were three-dimensional.
5. Fill your motif with lines similar to its own lines, straight and angular or soft and curving.
6. Fill your shape with lines that are dissimilar to its own lines, such as curves within the triangle.

22

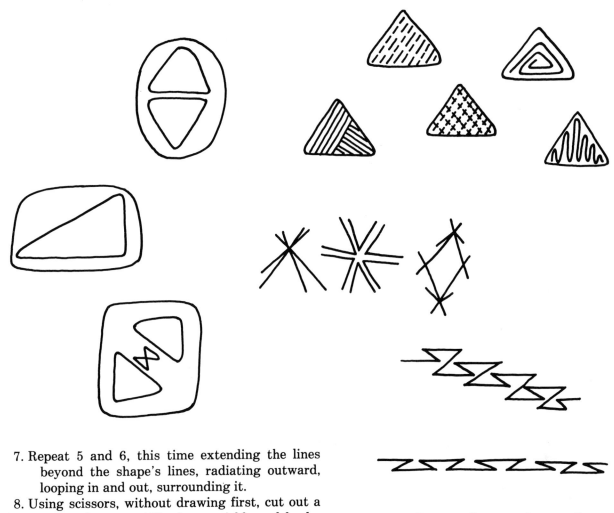

7. Repeat 5 and 6, this time extending the lines beyond the shape's lines, radiating outward, looping in and out, surrounding it.
8. Using scissors, without drawing first, cut out a series of your motif's shape quickly and freely. Try arranging the cut pieces together.
9. Quickly draw a series of free shapes, and place your motif within each.
10. Fill your motif with relaxed texture lines.
11. Separate the various parts of your motif, rearranging them if possible. For instance, the straight lines and angles of the triangle can be used.
12. Without taking your pen from the paper, try drawing a series of lines from your motif.

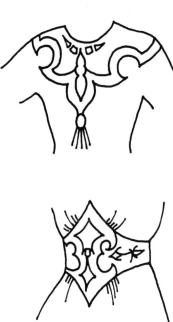

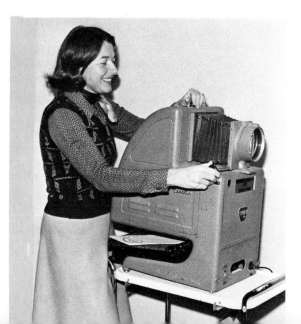

Maryann Pember using an opaque projector to determine scale of a design idea. She then can draw along the projected lines to make a pattern.

ENLARGING OR REDUCING

Only after I am satisfied with a design will I enlarge it to its final scale. I find it much easier to work with a fairly small sketch. If the first rough drawing is too small, I do resketch it to a comfortable working size. What is comfortable will differ from person to person. How complete you want your sketch notes is, again, a personal decision. I prefer getting the overall shapes and proportions worked out and leaving the actual stitch details to be filled in freely later. But some designs call for tighter planning than others. You might want to work with small sketches while getting your general concept mapped out and then draw in the final details after enlarging the sketches to scale.

Probably the simplest method of enlarging, and one that takes the least equipment, is that of using a grid and squared paper. Both the paper with your original sketch on it and a paper large enough to contain the enlarged motif should be squares. Mark or fold them into even, square segments, making the same number of folds or divisions on both the large and small paper. In each square of the large paper, draw only the lines that appear in each corresponding square of the original sketch. Work square by square until the entire design has been transferred, giving you your motif in the correct size. This enlargement can be cut as a pattern, traced, or transferred to your fabric—whatever method is needed for the technique you will be working in.

If your sketch is larger than the area you intend to embroider, you can reduce it by using the same grid method. Your sketch will be on the large paper, and you will transfer its lines to the squares of the small paper.

24

Some cities have photocopy services that will enlarge and/or reduce copy at a reasonable cost. Work larger than notebook size may need to be done a segment at a time. The pieces can be taped together later.

Projectors have become a part of our mechanized lives and can be helpful in enlarging sketches as well as in adapting ideas you've collected so they can become your motifs. An opaque projector is often available for short-term use at a nearby school. The image of any object (including objects not completely flat, such as plates or sea shells) placed on the tray of this type of machine will be projected onto a surface.

An important advantage to using any projector is the speed with which you can explore a shape in various sizes. The closer the projector is to a reflecting surface, the smaller the image will be; as the distance increases, the image becomes larger. Once you have settled on the right size, a paper can be taped onto the surface where the image is projected and then drawn on. You can sketch the reflected lines right through their light. Use a soft pencil or colored chalk. (Pens tend to balk if you try to use them on a vertical surface.) This technique can be especially helpful for a very large-scale project, such as a rug or enlarging a small motif to fit the length of a long skirt. Make only a rough sketch. Refine it later. Remember, the object is to adapt, not copy!

Try projecting the image against something other than a plain white flat area. For instance, if working toward a circular design, tack up a piece of paper with the right size circle drawn on it, varying the size and placement of the projected image for differing effects. Tissue pieces from your garment pattern can be taped to the wall, or even try projecting the image directly onto a person. Have someone dressed in something plain and light colored stand in front of the projector. Have the person move closer to or farther from the light, and watch the changes as the light plays over the body form. This is a good way for the slightly inhibited person to break away from thinking small.

Caftan showing good use of related motifs. Shell shapes, including real shells, merge with flowing, swirling lines, reminiscent of beaches. By Joanne Haldeman.

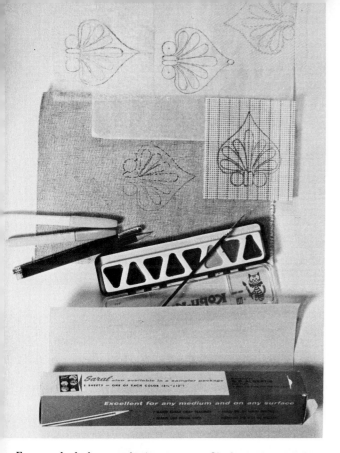

Four methods for transferring patterns. Clockwise from top left: fusible webbing, tracing paper, nylon net, waste canvas. The pattern in center is on linen; upper half is marked, through net, with permanent marker, lower half with watercolor. Child's watercolors, shown with 000 art brush, heat-transfer pencils and permanent markers, are useful, as is tracing or dressmaker's carbon, shown in roll form.

Stitching directly through marked nylon net, the net to be cut away later.

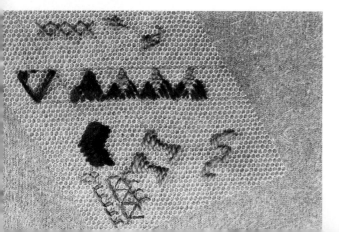

Marking Methods

Once you have your finished design worked out to scale on paper, you need to transfer it to the fabric itself. You can draw or trace it directly onto the fabric, using ruled or grid lines as guides. There are many other methods, and new products appear frequently. Some things to consider when choosing a method are: the fabric being used—its texture, color, and washability; the size and complexity of the motif itself; and your own working habits. No attempt is made to list every method, but here are some you might consider.

TRANSFER METHODS

To use dressmakers carbon, work on a firm surface and lay your fabric flat. Place the dressmakers carbon in position, lay your tracing or drawing on top of it, and mark each line of the motif firmly and repeatedly, peeking under to see if enough pressure is being applied. Heat-transfer pencils may be used instead of dressmakers carbon. Use a color that will contrast with your fabric, and mark repeatedly over your tracing lines. Turn this marked surface against your fabric, and press it with a dry, warm iron until the color transfers. In marking, sufficient pencil build-up must be made for your lines to transfer to the cloth. Be aware that your transferred motif will appear in reverse from your original drawing. Children's crayons can also be heat-transferred in much the same way but do not wash away. Washability of the pencils varies—as always, test to be sure.

26

TEMPLATES

Cut paper shapes can be placed on the fabric. Baste or stitch around them and remove. The stitching adds further embellishment to your design. Straight lines can be worked along Scotch tape taped directly on your cloth. Magic transparent tape (Scotch) can be marked quickly at measured intervals to assure even spacing of stitches along your straight line.

NYLON NET

Place the net over your drawing and trace it with a permanent marker. Then place the net on the fabric and draw over the tracing lines with the marker. Your fabric will be marked directly through the mesh. You can stitch directly through net for certain types of stitching and cut it away after completing the work. Erica Wilson suggests that fusible webbing can be used for direct tracing and basted into position on the fabric. Stitching can then be worked directly through both the marked webbing and the cloth beneath it. After the embroidery is complete, the webbing can be carefully cut away. (Remember to always keep the webbing away from direct contact with your hot iron.)

WASTE CANVAS

Trace directly onto waste canvas, baste into position, and stitch through both the canvas and the fabric beneath. The canvas can then be unraveled and pulled from the stitching. This method will leave the stitches slightly raised on most fabrics. Any counted-thread stitches are applicable. Canvas can be dampened, which weakens the sizing and makes unraveling easier. (Do not try to use interlocked canvas.)

BASTING THREADS

Trace the motif onto tissue paper. Position this on your cloth, and baste along the tracing lines through both cloth and paper. The paper can then be carefully torn away, leaving basting lines for guides.

Cut-paper rock shapes arranged on dress-pattern shape, traced onto monocanvas, and basted onto a black wool knit. Stitches are worked through both canvas and fabric; then the canvas is carefully removed.

Cut paper pinned in place to be stitched around.

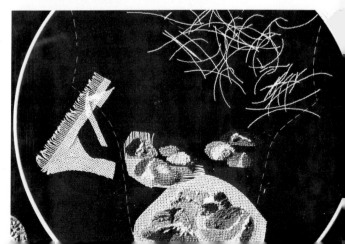

Skirt by Neva in her own technique of Cut-Away Appliqué, a method patented by her in 1966.

MARKING TOOLS

Marking methods require marking tools. Dressmakers carbon, heat transfers, and basting are each method and marker at once. Marking tools for other methods include tailors chalk and pencils, water-soluable pens and pencils meant for use on cloth, and permanent markers (which come in a wide variety of colors). Lassie Wittman recommends soap slivers, especially for long, straight lines.

Colorfastness of markers varies and, again, should be tested. There is a difference between washability and bleeding. A line may or may not wash out of your fabric. It can be covered with stitches but may bleed color into some of the fibers of your embroidery. Test by washing all combinations. Labels can be guides, but they do not eliminate the need for testing.

One problem with many pencils, chalk, and soap lines is that they rub off with frequent handling. It helps to transfer only part of the motif at a time, stitch that, then mark and stitch the next area. I often reinforce tracing-carbon lines, using a child's set of paints from the neighborhood drugstore but applied with a very fine 000 brush from the art supply. A thinner line can be drawn with this tiny brush than with any other marker I know, and with less drag on the cloth. On most fabrics, not enough paint is left to bleed during cleaning (but I do test first). A thinned-down acrylic paint can be used in the same way and would be permanent.

Long coat of Guatemalan handwoven stripe, lined in a light-weight cotton batik. By Melinda Phillips.

Detail of chain stitch worked in linen thread.

Vest of synthetic brushed velvet. The entire lower section has a stem-stitched grid worked over the patchwork, which is mostly Thai silks. By Mary Ann Spawn.

Patchwork and grid detail of vest. Photo and photo at left by Doug Spawn.

Freely worked flowers cascade over sleeves of a blouse of Swiss cotton. Placed high on one sleeve, low on the other, the flowers are worked in DMC cottons, perle and stranded, of silk and Japanese gold. Stitchery and photo by Jacqueline Enthoven.

Detail of Ultrasuede vest. Some of the other stitches are French and bullion knots for the flower centers, wrapped chain stitching for the stems, and padded detached buttonhole in Paternayan wool for the calyxes. Photo and photo above, right, are courtesy of the artist.

Bright flowers of detached knotted buttonhole of #5 DMC perle cotton highlight Vima Micheli's Ultrasuede vest and matching skirt.

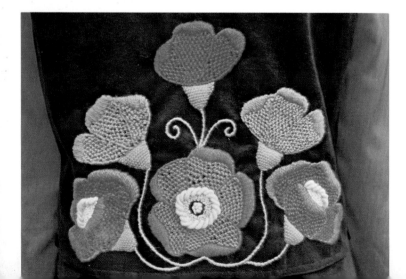

Grape Cape with stuffed velveteen grapes and lined leaves partially attached to a cape of navy wool. Tendrils are velveteen cording over wire. The grape design is repeated by machine embroidery in the raspberry satin lining. Stitchery and photo by Eleanor Van de Water.

A yoke extending partway down a sleeve is predominately embellished with shi sha and feather stitches. By Mary Ann Spawn.

Dress of striped cotton with embellished yoke. The randomly worked fly stitch of Danish cotton was occasionally filled with the closed buttonhole in colors of the stripe. By the author.

Dress of crisp cotton-silk with Ultrasuede appliqué embellished with stitches. Design influenced by Akha jacket.

(Left) *Young woman of the Meo hill tribe of northern Thailand working on a cross-stitch band to insert in a skirt typical of her tribe. She works from the back of the cloth, rather than from the front.*

(Right) *Back panel of a woman's jacket, from the Akha tribe of Burma, with appliqué and stitching on the handwoven cotton.*

Teneriffe wheels and tassels found in a thieves' market were incorporated in a lacy yoke of needle lace on hand loomed fabric from India. By Helen Richards.

Shells and shapes from the sea flow from shoulder to waist on a dress by Louise Schwab. Buttons were made of cowrie shells with backs attached to them.

Freely worked mosaic of silks highlighted by butterflies. Clusters of flowers and leaves are worked in the bullion knot. By Mary Ann Spawn.

Needlepoint vest worked on #18 pink linen canvas chosen for suppleness. Edging is of jet bugle beads. By Jeannine Bowen.

Making the Garment

When making the garment yourself, it is often easiest to do embroidery before assembling and even, if possible, before completely cutting out. Lay the entire pattern out on your material and pin into place. Cut out pieces, except those that you plan to embroider. The embroidery pieces remain uncut, hopefully grouped together and pinned in place on the fabric. If not, leave as much fabric as possible around each piece wherever it is. Mark around each pattern piece with tailors chalk or basting. Mark a second line for the work area. Guide marks, such as buttonhole placement or pattern centers, should also be marked. Darts should be marked. Remove the paper pattern and mark the seam allowance. Now, before cutting out, mark and work the embroidery you have planned. One of two things may be done where seams will later be joined in the area of the embroidery. If the embroidery is not bulky, it can be worked right into the seam allowance, and the seams can be sewn through it. If the work is bulky, work close to, but not into, the seam allowance. After the seams are closed, the embroidery pattern can be carried across the finished seams.

If you work with your material in a frame or a hoop, you will need enough fabric to stretch over its edges. It will be easiest if the embroidery can be done before the garment pieces are cut out. It also works well if the pieces can be cut with enough material left around them to fit into the hoop. If the pieces must be cut out and are too small or the wrong shape to be held by the hoop, try basting them to muslin, cutting the muslin away from the underside in the working area.

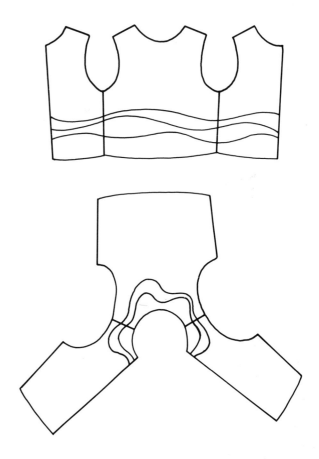

Garment seams may be partially joined to allow working a full design area.

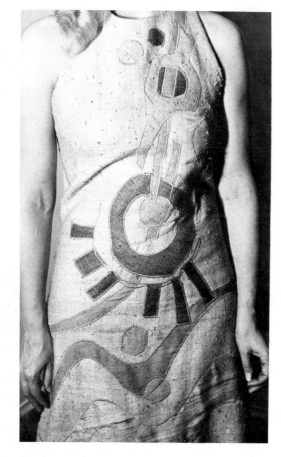

Machine appliqué of silk tussah. By Carol Sabiston.

An appliqué eagle spreads across the shoulders of a smock. By Katharine Ireys.

Fabrics that have a firm weave may need no hoop; or a small hoop might be used and moved repeatedly as work progresses. Stay-stitching cut pieces that will be worked is a good practice. Even when using a frame or hoop, embroidery can sometimes cause distortion. Check each piece against your paper pattern, and make any adjustments necessary before proceeding with the garment construction.

Sometimes it is necessary to put the garment together, at least partially, before embroidering. For instance, joining the shoulder seams of a garment but leaving the side and facing seams to be joined after embroidering allows you to work freely over an area. Linings should be added after working, but if your garment is not to be lined, use extra care at the back of your stitches. The inside of your garment must be neat enough to be practical. There should be no bulky knots or long threads dangling. Thread floats should be kept short so as not to catch on fingernails or zippers.

Embroidery can put extra strain on fabrics. Thin silks may hang best with a light muslin or nylon net interlining or interfacing under the areas to be embroidered. The stitches should go through both fabrics. Beading of any kind should certainly be supported firmly in this manner. The interlining is sometimes cut away after embroidering, leaving it under the embellished area only.

When embroidering on a finished garment, there are several preliminary steps that will make work a bit easier. Remove or release all linings around the area in which you will be working. If you want to stitch where there is a closed facing, such as a self-lined tie, release the seam for several inches so you can work. It can be blind-stitched together again when you finish. Small hoops can be bought that slip into narrow places like sleeves. A piece of cardboard can be cut to slide into sleeves or pockets to prevent your needle from picking up two layers of cloth at once.

Techniques

Each of the techniques of embroidery carries its own fabric and design possibilities in garments. We will talk about several, one at a time.

APPLIQUÉ

Appliqué is an efficient method for getting results quickly. It is an easy way to set up color or texture changes on a garment, to duplicate shapes, or to establish a decorative motif. Appliqué can be large or small, in a single motif or repeated units. It can be of one piece of fabric; or it can be of a group of fabrics, applied adjacent to one another or with some overlapping others.

Appliqué is essentially the application of one piece of fabric on top of another. The edges may or may not be turned under, according to the needs of the materials and the intended design. The holding stitches may be blind, running, or decorative. Traditionally, plain appliqué was most often stitched with the blind stitch or the running stitch, its edge turned under with your needle as you worked. The blind stitch gives a slight puffiness to the applied piece; the running stitch creates characteristic dimples along the stitch lines.

Any number of decorative stitches may be used instead of, or in addition to, the two stitches mentioned. Stitches that cross over the edge at angles can be especially effective: the blanket stitch, overcast stitch, satin, Cretan, cross stitch, herringbone, feather, fly stitches, or simply a random straight stitch. Chain, stem, and back stitching can all re-

Large-scale appliqué floral by Melinda Phillips. Coordinating stripes are sewn strips of fabric.

31

Brilliant, hand-dyed silks in appliquéd patchwork. By Melinda Phillips.

place the running stitch, and any of these might be threaded, whipped, or looped. Try the Pekinese stitch looped through the back stitch. The blanket stitch can be a base for a raised chain; a row of French knots or the Palestrina knot can add a beaded effect.

In addition to holding stitches, your total design may call for stitch embellishment. Major focal areas may be appliqué, or the appliqué may provide only the background for the stitches over and around it.

Machine-stitched appliqué has become a great favorite. Flat edges are often smoothly satin-stitched. Another machined holding-stitch technique is repeated vertical or horizontal overstitching of the flat, unturned edges with straight stitches.

There are three basic appliqué techniques: onlay, where fabric is applied over a ground fabric; inlay, where two fabrics are cut and butt-seamed together and the join covered with a couched thread or stitches; and reverse appliqué, where several pieces of material are layered, then cut through from the top to the successive layers to reveal the underlying fabrics. Reverse appliqué will be so designated. Inlay, most commonly used with very heavy fabrics, is not a common technique for clothing and is not discussed. When I refer to appliqué, I will be referring only to the onlay technique, the most common of the three.

The crisp body of some recent cotton blends, such as Concord's Kettle Cloth, is especially suited to appliqué stitching—hand or machine—and the blends have been a favorite of many. Applying print fabric, hand prints as well as commercial material, is a popular method of creating interesting embellishment. In the lining of the blue silk coat by Melinda Phillips, a variety of prints have been cut freely and juxtaposed with contrasting prints and sewn patchwork. The blind holding stitches are also the coat's quilting stitches, so the same shapes appear in the lining as on the blue silk. Print motifs can easily be cut and applied in less involved arrangements.

A wide variety of materials can be combined to create special effects, limited only by your imagination and the need to avoid potential cleaning problems. Try opaque appliqué on sheer materials, making sure that the combined weights will hang correctly. One texture can offset another for appliqué: a soft handweave, a velvet, or various pile weaves—including fake fur—against a plain or flat woven or knitted wool; shiny metallics highlighting a dressy crepe; synthetic leather with a woven fabric. In the suit by Barbara Trellis, the black Ultrasuede of the skirt is repeated in the facing and appliqué on the open-weave top. (Ultrasuede and metallics are both discussed later in the book.)

Another potential material for appliqué is embroidery that has once been part of something else. Not all "antique" garments belong in museums. Garments wear out unevenly, and beautiful old embroidery can be rescued and given new life as an appliqué on something for today.

Procedures

The amount of preplanning you prefer will influence your own approach. Some artists like to cut fabric shapes freely, pinning them into place as they go, arranging and rearranging until satisfied, then stitching them into place. In an interview, Norman Laliberté, a master of free appliqué used for banners, exclaimed, "Just let it happen with scissors. If you think bird, there's no way it can come out an elephant. . . you call your image and you can't pull away from it. . . cut freely, then refine—cut, and let the shape tell you what it is. . . a line is for paper; cutting into cloth is direct. . . just cut and go, shove your shapes around, this angle or another—something will happen."

A favorite device of good art teachers is to have students try working methods (or techniques or color choices) they do not ordinarily use. While you may not approach Laliberté's spontaneous, exuberant freedom, you might find that freely cutting and arranging shapes helps you to achieve a new look to your work.

Yet some ideas can only be carried out by careful planning and by refining your design before you start to work. Use the design-planning and transfer methods already discussed. If

Hand-quilted coat of blue hand-dyed silk. The quilting pattern is determined by the mélange of prints cut and freely arranged, appliquéd, and quilted. By Melinda Phillips.

Henna-colored top of Kettle Cloth with appliquéd circles of the garment fabric used with tie-dyed and brayer-printed fabrics. Colors of printed fabrics are repeated in the stitching, using a "detour" design technique. The design area continues over the shoulder and partway down the back and is repeated on the legs of matching pants. By Helen Richards.

(Opposite page) *Puffy squares on appliquéd patchwork are described on page 36.*

you are working with an unfamiliar fabric, test it by cutting out a small shape which has about the same angles and curves as your planned motif. See how easily it handles, how much fraying there is, whether or not it needs its edges turned under, what effects various stitches produce. If there seems to be difficulty with the necessary turnbacks, try simplifying your shape by eliminating some curves or angles. Know what your material will do before you start working your design.

Cut your shapes around a paper pattern or along lines transferred to, or drawn directly on, the fabric. Cut appliqué pieces so the grain direction of their fabric is the same as that of the fabric under them; this keeps them lying smoothly. If the edges are to be turned under, add 3/8-inch seam allowance all around. Clip edges and angles to allow the turnback to lie flat. Some like to finger-press this turnback, but do not iron it. This flattens the folded edge too severely, destroying the softer, three-dimensional look characteristic of appliqué. If the edges are not to be turned under, more intricate, angular shapes are possible.

Pin or baste your shapes into position on their ground fabric. If there are several parts or colors of the design to be cut and placed individually, consider their order and which ones will overlap their neighbors. When such overlapping occurs, the edges that lie beneath the upper fabric should not be turned under, since this creates a visible ridge. For a motif with several components that must be placed precisely, Anne Dyer of England suggests making two tracings of your design. Cut one into pattern pieces, and leave the second intact. After cutting out the fabric pieces, pin each in place to the back of the intact tracing. This can then be placed on your garment fabric and each piece repinned, this time in its correct position on the garment.

Holding stitches can be worked with the piece either pinned or basted into position. Basting stitches should be done in random rows of long running stitches back and forth across the face of your piece, and they should always stop ½-inch short of the edge to leave room for turning under. A basting line that only runs parallel to the edge of your work will not keep the piece as flat as the random basting does.

"Basting" can also be accomplished on some fabrics by using iron-on fusible webbing. Small snippets of the webbing can be placed at several points under a piece and bonded with a hot iron. Another way to use the webbing is to cut it into the shape of your piece. Trim a slight edge off the entire perimeter so no webbing protrudes from under your cut piece. Now cut away the center of the webbing, leaving a 3/16- to 1/4-inch ring of bonding. This will hold the entire edge of your piece, and a scrap of webbing will hold the center. Follow brand directions for bonding with a hot iron. (A dampened, folded paper towel can provide extra steam when bonding. Mark its upper side so that you always use the towel with the same side down. This prevents stray bits of web from touching your iron.) Bonded edges will not fray, eliminating the need to turn under. Holding stitches are still necessary and decorative stitches may be added. To bond any shape entirely is likely to cause unwanted stiffness. While partial bonding is less stiff, it is still not desirable for all fabrics—test.

Appliqué variations

The appliqué we have talked about lends itself to variations, mainly in the treatment of its edges: whether or not to turn under; what kind of holding and/or decorative stitches will provide the effect you want; and whether your appliqué is to be a major or minor part of the design. But always the appliqué was used flat against its ground. Three-dimensional effects are also possible if you stuff or pad the pieces before they are completely sewn down. Or they can be lined or finished in such a way that they need be only partially attached rather than sewn completely flat. One way to do this is like making a pillow casing. Cut two fabric pieces of your design shape (one piece may be a lighter-weight lining). With right sides together, sew close to the edge along the perimeter, leaving an opening large enough to allow you to pull the casing right side out. The size of the opening will depend on the weight of the fabric and the size of the piece; you may

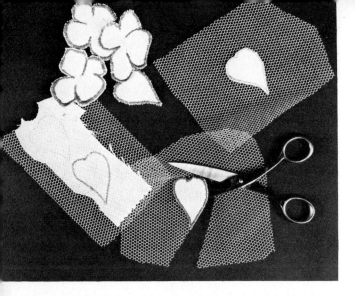

Appliqué need not be entirely attached to a ground fabric. (Top) Floral shapes are given a finished edge, backed with net, and will be only partially attached as part of a design. (Bottom) Padded velvet grapes, double-faced leaves, and tendrils of cord inserted with wire add dimensional appliqué to "Grape Cape." By Eleanor Van de Water.

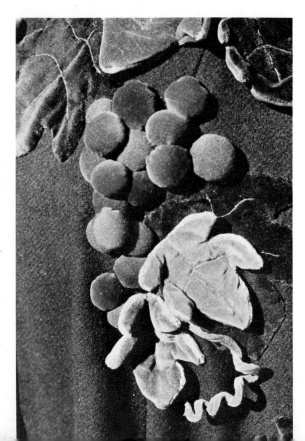

wish to reach inside to push the seam completely to its edge. Stuffing or padding may be added, giving the piece depth. Press the casing lightly and then blind-stitch the opening. The piece is ready to attach, either completely or partially.

Another variation is to finish the edges with a satin stitch, by machine or hand. In the detached flowers shown, the following method is used. First, the motif pieces are drawn on the wrong side of the fabric. A 6-inch square of nylon net is cut for each piece and laid over the drawn motif. Narrow zig-zag stitching is done along the drawn line through both the net and the fabric. The excess fabric is then cut away very close to the stitching line, care being taken not to cut the stitches or the nylon net. This leaves you with your design shape stitched to a large enough square of net to hold and guide under the machine needle. The net could be cut large enough for a hoop, if you prefer. (If the fabric frays easily, you might want to run a very thin line of thinned glue or nail polish just along the cut edge.) Then, holding the net flat and taut, sew around the edge with a machine satin stitch. Work wide enough to cover the underlying zigzag. You can also finish the edge by hand, using satin, buttonhole, or any covering stitch. The net can then be carefully cut away, leaving the nicely finished edge. This is an easy way to obtain a smooth edge. The net backing adds crispness and body.

Mary Ann Spawn creates puffy squares that are especially effective in her appliquéd patchwork. She uses rectangles of decorator's velvet, usually on a ground of velvet of the same weight, and each piece is pinned and the edges turned under and blind-stitched into position. A decorative row of stem stitching is worked parallel to and outside the completed edge. Then, rather than adding further rows out away from the piece, she works in, adding row upon row of stem stitches crowding toward the center of the patch. With each row, the patch develops more puffiness. An example of this can be seen on the preceding page.

Meo village in northern Thailand. Bottom bands on pleated skirts are solidly worked cross stitch. Girl on left is working on a narrow cross-stitch band.

Reverse appliqué

Reverse appliqué involves the layering of fabrics cut to the same size, usually in two to five layers, each of a different color. Starting at the top, the motif is cut through one layer at a time until you reach the bottom layer, which remains uncut.

Many people know of this technique as used for molas by the Cuna Indians of the San Blas Islands. But it is also used in other cultures. The Meo hill tribes, found in the mountainous areas of Southeast Asia, do beautiful reverse appliqué with fine cuts that would be difficult to duplicate. The examples shown were bought at a night market of open stalls in Chiang Mai, in northern Thailand, where the surrounding hill tribes come to trade.

If you do a reverse appliqué of three layers, you stack all three and baste them together along the edge with large running stitches. Draw or transfer your design shapes onto the

Meo woman working on treadle sewing machine outside her home.

37

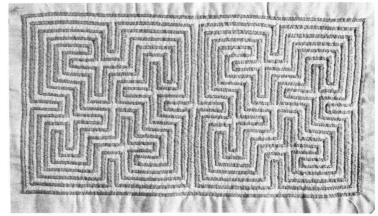

top layer. With small, sharp scissors, cut just inside your design lines, leaving enough fabric to turn back.

The next step varies. Some prefer to turn and blind-stitch each layer as it is cut, starting with the top layer. Design lines of the lower layers are then confined by the lines already sewn. Most contemporary artists do *all* of their cutting in *all* layers before they finish stitching anything. Then they start at the lowest layer to be sewn (second from the bottom, as the bottom layer remains uncut) and work up. This is a freer approach because you are able to overlap the edges in a variety of directions before the layers are sewn down.

It is also possible to insert a small patch of color in a single area rather than as a whole layer. Several colors can be inserted as patches, which greatly increases the color range without added bulk.

Barbara Summer in a dress featuring a design derived from her own profile and worked in layered appliqué. Design lines are extended outward from the insert and over the garment, unifying the whole.

Layered appliqué

Barbara Summer works a type of reverse appliqué by machine and calls it *layered* applique because, while it looks similar to reverse appliqué, this has a flatter appearance. The layers are basted together, and the design shapes are drawn or transferred in *reverse* on the wrong side of the bottom layer. (If drawn on the top layer, portions of the design lines would be lost as each layer is cut.) Working from the design shapes on the bottom, sew around all lines that enclose the color areas of the top layer, using a medium width, slightly open zigzag machine stitch. Next, from the top, trim away all areas which will not be this color. Repeat sewing from the back and trimming from the front until the shapes of all layers are complete. (Change thread color for each color change of fabric.) Now, cover all trimmed edges with a wide satin stitch in each fabric color, starting with the second layer from the bottom. Contrasting thread colors may be used instead, giving the appearance of additional color layers. Barbara is shown in a dress on which this technique was used, and her more detailed description of the technique appeared in the November 1978 issue of the *Flying Needle* magazine, published by the National Standards Council of American Embroiderers.

While Barbara's method evolved individually out of her own work, it is similar to a technique devised and patented in 1966 by Neva, under the trade name Cut-Away-Applique. In some of her designs, Neva uses canvas as the bottom layer, with the result that the needlepoint design is surrounded by fabric layers for a big effect that will work up quickly. A skirt showing her method is on page 28.

39

Silk pendants, 2 to 2½ inches in diameter, demonstrate how even a small touch of fine embroidery can create a focus of interest. By Mary Ann Spawn.

THE SMALL TOUCH

A small piece of embroidery can be intricate, can take a long time to make, and can be of the highest quality. Yet a small piece of even the finest work can be lost if the total garment has not been planned to show it to its best advantage. Make a little go a long way. (This is a good practice with large motifs, too, just not quite as necessary.) This can be done by using contrasts, highlighting the area containing the embroidery, extending lines of the design area outside the area itself, or doing the unexpected.

The unexpected

An embroidered bee set at a cocky angle on your upper sleeve—or above your hip in the back—will catch the eye more quickly than the same bee placed on your collar. Why? Because a nice little touch on the collar can be expected, but the eye is not prepared for the other. Cut the shape of your planned motif out of cloth similar to the color of your finished design, and place it on various spots of your garment while standing in front of a mirror. Constance Howard has said that every design needs a surprise, but not a shock. Look for the way your small touch can be a surprise. Don't assume symmetry. The majority of garments are made with the right side matching the left. Try for variations. Jacqueline Enthoven is fond of working an area of flowers high on one sleeve, low on the other. Again, the eye enjoys the unexpected.

40

Front and back view of a rust jersey dress falling from a yoke of cotton that has been "painted" with dye and freely embellished with stitches. By Mary Ann Spawn.

Contrast

Good design is built on contrasts—of color and its value, texture, line. In general, warmer, brighter colors advance and look larger. Cools and neutrals recede and look smaller. A small area of a bright color or of complex lines will balance a large area of neutral color or more restful lines. Make some of these principles work for you. They provide keys to better design. Keep the area surrounding your intricate embellishment low-keyed, in muted or neutral colors, or a color closely matching the underlying garment, and increase the intensity of the color as you get nearer your prized center of interest. This is not to say that your "jewel" of embroidery must be worked in bright reds and pinks. Only that, while it should relate closely to its surrounding hue, the strength of its color interest should draw the eye to it. Other eye catchers such as beads, cabochon stones, shi sha glass, metallic threads, and tassels can be added to help create this focal point.

Highlighting

A yoke, sleeve, cuff, panel—any single area created by the garment seams—can be cut in a contrasting fabric to highlight any embellishment. An inset yoke of a different color than the rest of the dress will attract your eye to the beautiful bit of embroidery that you have sewn there.

Areas can be highlighted by appliqué: bib, collar, or yoke shapes, perhaps with curving, decorative edges; wide bands of various widths running vertically or horizontally; or a large shape, compatible with the motif shape, extending the focal area. Highlighting can also be achieved by surrounding the design area with stitches or couched cords or threads, planned both in color and texture to support the central motif, not to compete with it. (If the surrounding area becomes

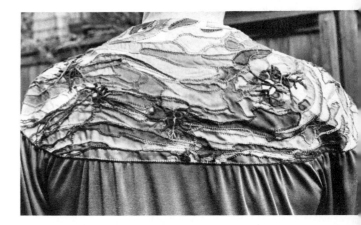

41

Traditional technique of tatting, in French cotton thread, applied and stitched in a contemporary manner to a polyester store-bought shirt. Careful tacking of each picot permits machine washing and drying without need for pressing. By Helen Richards.

equal in impact to the design area itself, then a new, larger motif has been created. This, obviously, can be desirable at times, but we are talking now about the small touch.)

Certain style/fabric combinations use the cut and hang of the fabric itself to establish a focal point. Soft knits, such as Qiana, light-weight sheers, and crepe de Chine are designed to fall from a specific point with graceful fullness. This point or small area where the fullness originates is often a flat yoke piece, whether at the neck, shoulders, or waist. A small amount of embroidery on that flat apex has every fold of the cloth leading up to it—a powerful focus. You might want to line the dress fabric in that area with muslin and work directly through both layers. It is also possible for that piece to be made of a fabric different from the rest of the garment—perhaps canvas (worked in silk) or a fabric more easily embroidered than the dress fabric.

Extending lines

Bringing stitch lines out of your embroidery and continuing them into their surroundings can attract the eye toward your motif. Barbara Summer's dress of layered appliqué is a good example of this. The eye moves easily to the appliqué areas from the dress and the other design area because of the extending lines. Any linear element of your design can be extended—perhaps one of them, perhaps several. Ribbons or other color bands can also be used to extend color for short or long distances.

VESTS

I've talked about ways to increase the impact of a small amount of embroidery because, often, the small touch may be a stitcher's first venture into using embroidery skill. Also, the embroidery of many who do beautiful but tiny and fine work is not noticed as much as it should be. The methods of drawing attention to an idea are essentially meant to work toward accomplishing total garment design. In total design, the garment itself becomes the perimeter of your planning.

A vest is a good first project for total design. The shape can be kept flat and simple, and the size is moderate—big enough to establish a strong design with almost any technique, but small enough to keep the design workable.

Patterns can be bought for a large variety of vest shapes. Favorite shapes among stitchers tend to be the bolero, the straight vest, and the vest composed of rectangular panels in front and back, joined by underarm pieces. All three are simple cuts and do not get involved with pockets, deep darts, or fastenings. Stitchery can be completed before assembling or after shoulder *or* side seams are joined (not both). The latter enables you to work across the full design area. Edges can be bound, or faced and lined. Vests generally should be lined, as the inside is likely to be visible at times.

These are three good shapes to start with; they offer good working spaces and few problems to contend with. But it is not difficult to develop the ability to approach your total design idea with no pre-imposed shape in mind. Shape is not limited to standard shapes. Choose a pattern which best suits your design. Cut it in muslin and baste it together. Cut

43

Vest of cotton muslin, bleached by artist. Trapunto design taken from rubbing of a coal-hole cover in London. Rubbings were done directly on cloth. Design can be traced onto cotton organza, which is then used both as the backing and as a stitching guide. By Joan Schulze.

Tom Lorenson in vest embellished with shi sha. By Eve Lorenson.

your motif shape in muslin also. Move it around on the vest, trying various positions, including extending beyond garment edges. The contour of your design could become your edge shape—a rounded petal edge for a flower might extend as a closing flap. Think of other edge changes that would add interest. After all, they don't have to be straight. They could be scalloped, jagged, or wavy. They could be cut high in front and dip in the back. Cut strips of muslin in whatever shapes seem worth trying. After you decide on an edge, baste it into position. When all modifications have been planned and are sewn into position, release the seams of your muslin vest, and use these modified shapes as your cutting design.

The ivory wool vest by Ginger Carter is cut with a diagonal lower edge. Being short, she felt that the usual straight lines cut her height and were not flattering. The upsweep of the cut is reinforced by the upward lines of the leaves of machine embroidery. The circles and bird are of chiffon overlays with hand and machine embellishments. All stitching—hand, machine, and appliqué—is in tones of red, from pale pinks through rusts to maroon. (Tiny touches of turquoise utilize the artist's device of adding punch to a color by using small amounts of its complement.)

Vests can be made in a variety of styles, materials, and design concepts. Each vest develops its own character, and that character may be altered by what is worn under it. One vest may work equally well with tailored pants or over a swirling dress of Qiana. Notice the variety of the vests.

Tom Lorenson's vest is of pale gray wool gabardine sprinkled with shi sha and worked in tones of ruddy red. Tom's wife, Eve, found herself so enthusiastic after learning this technique from Jacqueline Enthoven that she could hardly wait to find something to put it on. Tom's suit was handy and the color was right; so she bravely grabbed it and started attaching the shi sha mirrors, working right through linings and facings. (After all, why waste time on taking out linings!) Luckily, Tom enjoyed the whole thing. When fashion made men's vests all the rage for ladies, Eve put her own outfit together—full, black silk pants, a flowing pink blouse, and Tom's vest—and feels very swish.

A reversible vest by John Schulze uses ribbon appliqué on one side and large-scale drawn-thread work and free embroidery on the other. The quilted leaf vest is also by Joan; it's printed in fall tones on beige linen and machine quilted. Her trapunto vest is one of a series done from motifs gathered while on a trip to London.

The vest by Maggie Turner is of an ivory cotton blend. The meandering lines of the free Italian quilting create flowing spaces, some of which are stuffed, as in trapunto. This vest was made in two sections. In order to keep the shoulder area fitting smoothly without bulk, the lower padded area was worked separately, then trimmed to the resulting curved lines, and blind-stitched to the flat shoulder piece.

The short bolero vest by Louise Schwab is needlepoint, in a paisley pattern, trimmed with braid. Some of the paisley shapes were repeated around the skirt hem. The needlepoint stitches were worked through both canvas and the black wool of the skirt. When the needlepoint was completed, the canvas threads were removed, thread by thread, leaving the stitches directly on the wool.

Another vest by Louise Schwab is made of patchwork of approximately twelve colors of Ultrasuede. Louise's dressmaker has found that her clients object to pockets inserted into the side seams of Ultrasuede garments, as they create extra and unwanted bulk at the hip area. Many of her alterations involve removing such pockets and have left her with a drawerful of discarded Ultrasuede pockets. Louise put some of them to use. She cut her vest pattern in a bondable interfacing material—fabric backed with an iron-on bonding agent. The Ultrasuede pieces were arranged and cut to fit together in the patchwork shapes, basted on, then bonded onto the interfacing. Next, decorative silk holding stitches were worked on every piece. The vest pieces were finally assembled and washable lining was added, in keeping with the washability of Ultrasuede.

Another Ultrasuede vest, in green with a matching skirt, has a canvas border; so does the skirt. It is worked in green and white in a striking combination by Julia M. Goetsch.

(Top) *Appliquéd patchwork vest of Ultrasuede in a crazy-quilt pattern with embroidered accents.* (Bottom) *Needlepoint bolero with paisley detail repeated as a border, using waste canvas, on the black wool skirt. Both by Lousie Schwab.*

Ginger Carter in shaped vest of white polyester embroidered by both machine and hand stitching.

White muslin vest with freely worked trapunto. By Maggie Turner.

Green Ultrasuede vest with canvas inset. By Julia M. Goetsch.

(Clockwise, starting above) *Barbara Trellis in a suit of white wool with black Ultrasuede for skirt, front facing, and appliqué on sleeves. Canvas bib highlights caftan of camel-colored knit. By Barbara Trellis. Rayon, velvet, and linen threads combine for texture variation. Jo Reimer in a caftan with panels of reverse appliqué bordered by Seminole patchwork. Tops with insets of canvas work by Joan Bessom. Upper part of dress embellished with stitched and dye-painted linear design. By Eleanor Van de Water.*

(Top) *Purchased braid, held with decorative whip stitches, adds accent to black knit by Kirsch Misener.* (Bottom) *Purchased yarn braid, held in place with decorative stitches of the same yarn as was used for the hand-knit coat it is on. By Carol Schimanski. Courtesy of Ferne Cone.*

SURFACE STITCHERY

Surface stitchery is an embroidery stitch worked on the surface of any fabric. Some distinguish it from canvas work because with canvas the stitcher creates, as well as decorates, the fabric. Like a warp on a loom, canvas is not complete until filled with stitches. But the classifications can't be rigid—some of the softly colored linen canvases can easily have areas left unstitched. A distinction is also made between all counted-thread techniques, including canvas, and stitches that the craftsperson is free to move and turn at will on the fabric's surface. While names and categories can be an interesting study, I would guess that most beautiful work has been done with little regard for categories.

Scale, in my opinion, is the single most important influence on your choice of stitches. Unless you wish to spend a decade working on one exquisite dress, you must choose a technique which can cover the area to be embroidered within a reasonable time. As you look at each technique, consider the time it takes as well as its impact.

Couching

Couching is an excellent method for a big effect. Worked small, especially with fine silk or gold threads, it can hardly be considered fast. But if worked with heavier yarns or braids, it can go quickly, making long unbroken lines that can add a raised texture to your fabric.

In couching, a long thread is held to the surface of the fabric by smaller stitches crossing over it. Usually the holding stitches are of a second, finer thread than the thread being held. In some, such as the Bokhara or colcha stitch, or Romanian couching, the surface thread is held on the surface

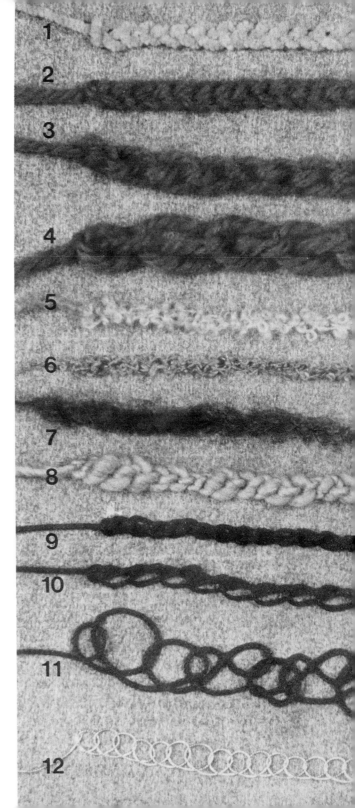

Single crochet in a variety of stitches (see text below).

by the return pass of the same thread emerging at intervals and crossing in ways characteristic to each stitch. The placement and amount of holding thread visible on the surface create various patterns.

Contemporary stitchers use a wide variety of yarns for both the couched and the couching thread. The blouse showing white lines of couching against a black knit is by Kirsch Misener. A textured braid was couched with an acrylic yarn of nearly the same color value, resulting in a wider line more firmly integrated with the knit than would have been true if the holding stitches were less apparent.

A single-crocheted chain makes an excellent braid to be couched. It works up quickly and can be made to exact length. Another advantage is that crocheted chains are much lighter and more flexible than most bought braids; so they cause little drag or bulk on the fabric. Change in yarn and stitch size can vary the braid width.

The sampler shows a variety of yarns worked up in this simple and quick manner. They have all been blind-stitched on for the best comparison, but any could be held by decorative stitches done in yarns—perhaps built out from both sides. These chains can be used as edgings, borders, trims, or to cover appliqué edges or seams.

From top to bottom: 1. Chenille. 2,3,4. Identical rug wool worked in three stitch sizes. 5,6. Looped novelty yarns. 7. Mohair blend. 8. Thick-and-thin wool. 9,10,11. Cording worked in three stitch sizes. Loops in 10 are pulled open and to one side for couching; 11 is couched with the loops falling randomly—some waiting to be filled with stitches, knots, or beads. 12. Christmas package cording couched with loops held to one side.

(Top) *Freely crocheted cord with accents of stitches and beads. By Doris Katz.* (Bottom) *Persian yarns couched on linen by machine zigzag stitching of clear nylon thread.*

The dress shown has two rows of crocheted chain being attached with matching yarn. The Scotch tape provides guides for keeping the line straight. Photo on the left shows a front detail of a coat by Doris Katz in which a freely crocheted cord, similar to number 11 shown on the sampler, was used. French knots, old silver Mexican beads, chain, and squared chain stitches embellish the free line.

Couched yarns can also be held by machine stitching. A simple, widely spaced zigzag was stitched over Persian yarns for the illustrated plaid. The machine was threaded with clear nylon filament, which added texture but not color to the wool yarns. Yarns can also be held by machine stitches that cross over them at wider intervals, such as a scallop stitch or one meant for blind hemming, each creating its own appearance and texture.

Ornate scrolls of couched braid can be seen on traditional garments from Yugoslavia and other Balkan countries. To do this technique, draw symmetrical curves on kraft or tissue paper or on fusible web (as described on page 27). A French curve can assist in drawing graceful curves. Baste this paper design in place on your garment; then baste the braid along the drawn lines, sewing through both the paper and the fabric. Now tear the paper away and blind-stitch the braid to finish.

An unbroken pencil line can set up other design possibilities for braid work, as suggested in the design exercises. By not taking the pencil from the paper, you are duplicating the flowing line of the braid. The stiffness and width of braids vary, as will the amount of curvature each will take and still remain flat and smooth. Play with your braid to determine its natural characteristics. Finish blind-stitching in place. While traditional braids were often a part of quite ornate and colorful embroidery and appliqué, they seldom were filled with embroidery embellishments themselves. But this is worth trying.

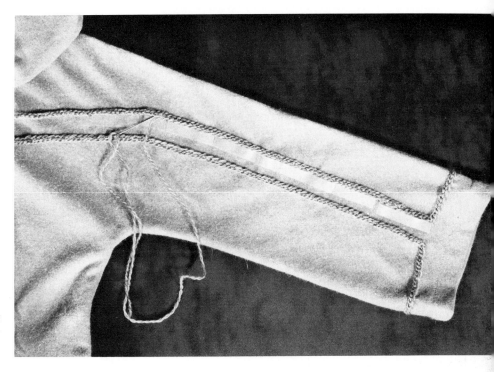

(Top) *Crocheted chain held with whipped stitches.* (Bottom) *Pinning braid in place as boundary for stitched free-form design.*

To do braid work in a contemporary and free manner, place your garment over a piece of shipping Styrofoam. Using long, ball-headed pins, loop and work with the braid, pinning in place whenever it seems to be right. Sometimes you will find it almost right but will still want to experiment. If so, trace or take a photo of the current arrangement. Or, before you start experimenting, slip a piece of paper under the garment but over the Styrofoam. After experimenting, slowly remove the pins, folding back the garment and marking from hole to hole on the paper as you take them away. This will leave you with a rough sketch of your arrangement, although you may find extra pinholes. This, or your photo or tracing, can serve as a pattern if you later want to repeat it. When you like the result of your experimenting, blind-stitch it into place, adding further embellishment if it fits. Borders with simple repeat loops are easily worked this way, need no pattern, and will take little reworking.

51

Parallel rows of stitches combine to form a border.

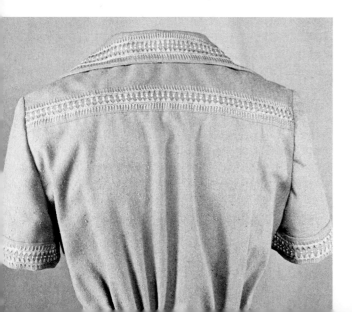

Borders

The long, unbroken lines of couching make good borders. The definition of border is the line along or parallel to the edge. For our use I would extend it to include any long lines of embellishment (along good construction seams or surrounding yokes) on the garment.

Perhaps the easiest way to establish a border with stitches is to combine rows of parallel stitches. They can be random, freely worked lines of feather, Cretan, or squared chain. The Palestrina knot makes a beautifully textured line, either winding or straight. Lines can weave with ease, crossing over one another or pausing for clusters of knots, flower shapes, or spider webs. Lines parting to go around a shape, coming together again after it has been passed, are sometimes called *detour* or *obstacle* design and are not limited to borders; they can flow over wider areas as well.

Another method of working borders is to do even, straight rows of evenly repeated stitches. Their effectiveness rests with the regularity of their repetition, and some manner of keeping stitches even is important. If the fabric allows, measuring stitch width and height by thread count is a guarantee to evenness. Even or regular weaves and medium to bulky knits usually allow you to follow their structure without markings. If this is not possible, it is advisable to set up some guides to keep the stitch line straight and the stitches at an even distance from each other. A see-through ruler is a helpful tool. Lines can be marked easily with this, using tailors chalk, pencils, washable or permanent pens, or soap slivers. You may want to make cross marks as well as length-

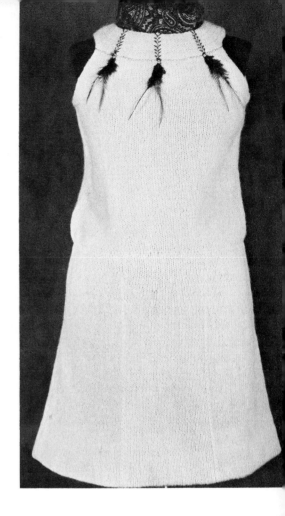

wise lines. On the blue dress, I drew grids with a fabric pencil, one section at a time, since it did rub off with handling. Sections were marked each time I moved the fabric forward on the frame.

A straight running stitch can be used as a guide. A favorite method of mine is using Scotch tape laid evenly along a see-through ruler. (Remember that if you use the Magic Scotch tape, you can mark on it easily at even intervals to space your stitches.) Most fabrics are not harmed by the tape, but as always, test. It should be removed from some fabrics, such as Ultrasuede, by pulling with, not against, the nap.

I have discussed borders in terms of multiple rows of parallel stitches. But a single line can highlight and set off an area, too. A touch of pizzazz was added to the dress knitted of ivory wool by Ferne Cone, author of *Knit with Style* and other books on knitting. Both edges of the neckpiece were stem-stitched in a textured, gold metallic thread. Ladders of fly stitches were whipped in the same gold thread, and the brown feathers added.

Still another good way to create a border is to build on purchased ribbon or decorative braid, or appliquéd bands of color. In the decorative braids shown, the holding stitches were worked in colors and stitches that fit the braid's own character. The cross-stitch diamonds are of the same blue and green found in the diamonds in the braid. The floral pattern is held by two rows of rambling feather stitches, and silk French knots and leaves are worked in colors from the center

53

Rows of stitches ending in attached feathers highlight neckline by Ferne Cone.

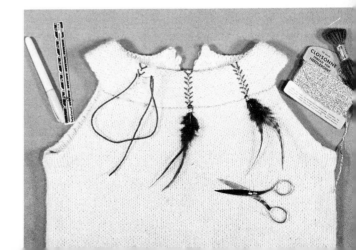

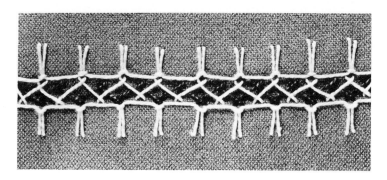

Cross stitches extend pattern shapes and colors of bought braid. Flower colors repeated in feather stitches of silk thread. Double herringbone bordered on each side by up-and-down buttonhole. Back yoke by Jo Reimer, showing parallel rows of various stitches bordering filled area of random buttonhole.

flowers. Both braids were "basted" in place with a narrow strip of fusible webbing.

Eventually, lines must turn. A mirror held at a 45-degree angle across a worked area of your border will show what the border will look like when turned 90 degrees. Move the mirror back and forth along the border (keep the same angle) and you will see how all the various stitches will look at the turn. Make quick sketch notes of how the threads meet, and refer to them later. A turn of any angle can be simulated by holding the mirror at half the wanted angle across the border.

Borders can be put to good use when reclaiming once-used garments. A moved seam or a let-out hem can leave lines that a border will cover. Worn areas that appear along pocket, sleeve, or neck edges are easily covered, as well as additionally protected from future wear, by rows of stitching. A garment that is too short can have a new piece of contrasting material and color inserted in a way that preserves good proportion. A new top can be put on an old skirt, or the skirt can be new and the top old. When these fabric changes occur, the two colors can be integrated by the use of stitch patterns across the color change. (Not all clothes can be reclaimed. Anne Dyer recommends that all clothing be bought with an eye toward future appliqué material!)

The coat shown has a new life today, largely with the help of borders. The coat was worn by Jill Nordfors for going away after her wedding. A beautiful English woolen, white and fleecy, it still had good lines, but the length was dated and some wear marks were beginning to appear at the neck and sleeve edges. Jill's mother, Mrs. Tom Denny, offered it

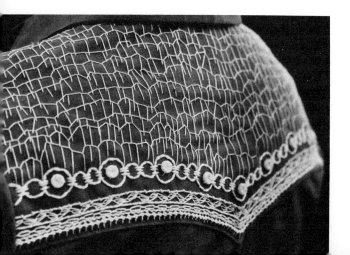

to me because of my current interest in updating garments—and it became a favorite project.

First the lining was removed and put away. Later I would use it as a pattern for cutting the new lining. Deciding on the right length was complicated somewhat by the spacing of the buttons. I pinned the hem at several lengths before finding the one that looked right with the spacing—a bit longer than I might otherwise have chosen, but still pleasing, I thought.

Had I not found a length that was compatible with the spacing, the existing buttonholes could have been whipped closed and new ones made. Than a wide band of stitching could have been worked right over the closed holes and around the new ones. The bulk of buttonholes should always be considered. These were bound buttonholes, so there were several layers of the heavy woolen. They probably would have shown under any but a heavily stitched band. Luckily, I could leave them in place.

I especially liked the seam lines of the coat and decided that decorative stitching along each seam would play them up. I found yarns of several weights and textures in an old-brass color that I liked and tried several stitch combinations on a scrap of fabric cut from the hem. The yarns were fairly bulky, in keeping with the weight of the coat material, and rows of Palestrina knot, stem stitch, and the up-and-down buttonhole soon ran over every seam line of the coat. The new lining matches the old-brass yarn, and horn buttons add to the vague Tyrolean feel of the "new coat."

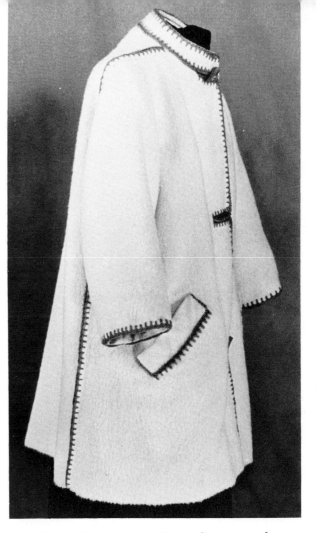

Coat of white English fleece with seam lines accented.

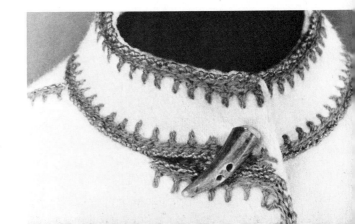

Helen Schwartz in tunic of even-weave rayon with motif, outlined in Florentine embroidery, surrounding patterns of blackwork. Motif designed and worked by Carol Frumhoff.

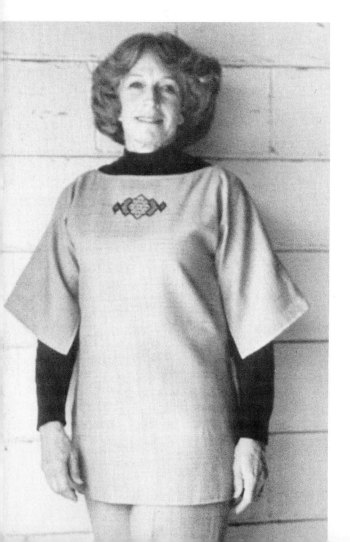

Counted-thread stitches

Counted-thread stitches are among the oldest types of stitching found and are enjoying a new popularity. Many stitches fall into this category, common ones being various forms of the cross stitch, blackwork, Holbein or double running, and darning stitches. Many of these counted-thread techniques use the open ground as part of the design itself. All canvas stitches depend on thread count, but in canvas work, the entire ground is usually covered.

Carol Frumhoff used the Florentine stitch (usually worked on canvas) as the outline of a motif on even-weave rayon, doubling its width every second row of holes. The number of strands was increased as the space became wider. Each shape was filled with blackwork. The garment was made and is modeled by Helen Schwartz.

Both Florentine and blackwork have great potential for clothing. The richness of Florentine, whether on counted thread or canvas, will combine well with a number of contrasting fabrics. Blackwork has been used for clothing for centuries, largely on soft, white linens. Ideas are just waiting to be updated and used with imagination.

Darning stitches: Konavlian

Darning stitches, especially pattern darning, are an intriguing technique. Using the very simplest of stitches, but in a highly controlled count, patterns of great beauty can be achieved. Leslie Mooers has researched and collected approximately one hundred different patterns of pattern darning developed along the Dalmatian coast in the valley of Konavli in Yugoslavia. This Konavlian embroidery falls into about six categories and is done on an even-weave fabric, the threads of which progress in a precise mathematical order. The patterns are worked from the back with a needle at a 45-degree angle, and several strokes of the pattern are formed in one manipulation. Thread ends are hidden because all work must be reversible. To judge work, it is traditional to hold it up to the light; in fine pieces, the embroidered areas totally block the light.

Cross stitches

The cross stitch is both one of the oldest and one of the most universal of stitches. Actually, numerous stitches are loosely called cross. Some are worked on the square with great precision; others are less formal.

Much of the cross-stitched peasant work from all over Europe has long been familiar to stitchers. But as our interest in the world's needlework expands, we are seeing many samples from other areas. The rural cotton embroideries of China, largely in cross stitch, date from 618 A.D. and are the subject of a book by Muriel Baker and Margaret Lunt (*Blue and White: the Cotton Embroideries of Rural China*, Scribners, 1977). The hill tribes of the mountainous regions of Southeast Asia (who originally migrated from China and whose cultural orgins are Chinese) still utilize cross-stitch patterns for their clothing. Young girls of five and six are taught to stitch, always working from the back of the cloth rather than the front, as we are accustomed to do. One tribe, the Yao, now uses more than fifty symbolic shapes, evolved from five of earlier years. Each girl is taught technique and the meaning of the symbols and then is expected to design her own work by adapting the symbols in a personal way. The marriageability of a girl is influenced by her ability with colors and designs.

The Meo tribes share many customs with the Chinese, one of which is the custom of wearing all new clothes for their new year festivities. Women of all ages can be seen in the vil-

Konavlian embroidery. By Leslie Mooers.

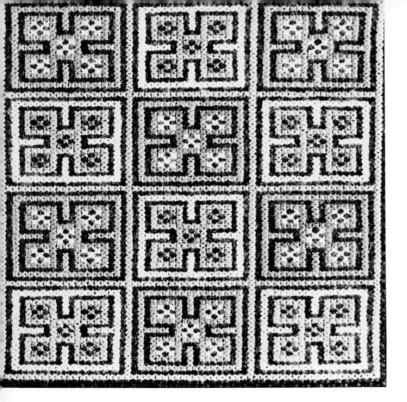

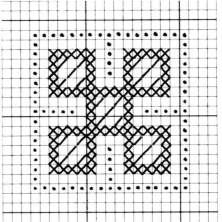

Cross-stitch patterns from hill tribes of northern Thailand. The stitch count is even in each direction and would result in a square pattern, as graphed, if worked on an even weave. Three of these examples are on a cotton of uneven thread count, resulting in rectangles instead.

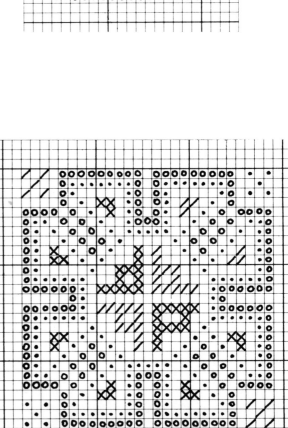

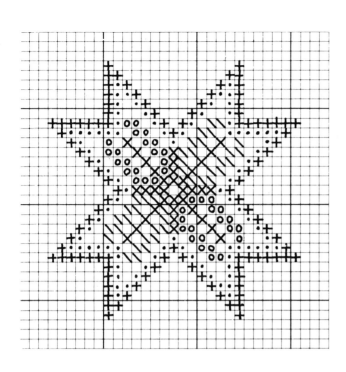

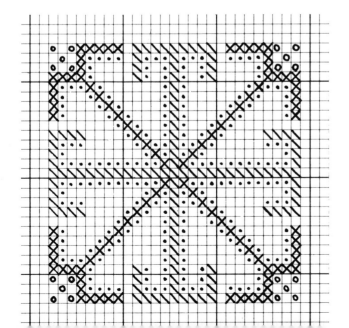

Shirt with cross-stitch and pulled-thread work on even-weave cotton. Made in Hong Kong.

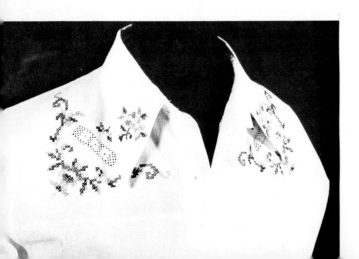

lage, working on batik, appliqué, cross stitch, and sewing. We saw no one wearing glasses (and no gray hair). Graphs of some of the Meo designs are shown. They show the correct stitch count, but the results are squares rather than rectangles as pictured, because these pieces were done on a 16-by-22-count black cloth rather than an even weave. We saw other work in the area on even weave, but it was not as fine a weave as these. The white piece is worked on even weave of 32 count. These pieces were also bought at the market in Chiang Mai in northern Thailand.

The cross-stitched blouse with pulled-thread work was bought in this country but made in Hong Kong (again, the Chinese heritage). The interesting thing about this blouse is that it has been made from two different fabrics. The embroidery has been done on a cotton of 75 thread count; the rest of the blouse is a cotton of 80 thread count. One wonders if the embroidery was originally worked to be something other than this blouse. I have seen cotton knit shirts, again from Hong Kong, with shoulder yokes of what appeared to be embroidered handkerchiefs. Combining fabrics is an important technique to consider for your own work. It is entirely possible to have any area—yokes, insets, collars, cuffs— made of a fabric different from the rest of the garment. If the texture and color are not too dissimilar, the difference is hardly noticeable; yet it can provide areas to support counted-thread, canvas, or other work that requires special grounds. On the other hand, the fabrics may contrast quite noticeably to draw attention to the embroidery.

A blouse from Athens is of rayon semi-sheer with the cross-stitched motifs in honey and brown. The cross stitch has been worked over a fine canvas which has been removed, leaving the stitches directly on the rayon. Every stitch on

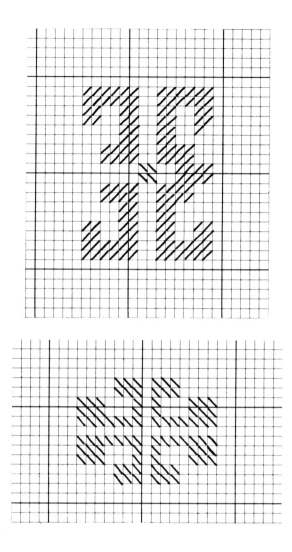

this blouse was made by hand, including the seams, which were held by a running stitch and then worked in a decorative stitch on the outside.

A tunic from Afghanistan is of rough handwoven cottons with bands of cross stitch in simple but effective motifs. Tabards, long or short, provide a good garment shape for embroidery work. Like vests, they can be worked flat, are of a moderate size, and are likely to go with a variety of clothing—or with new styles as they come along.

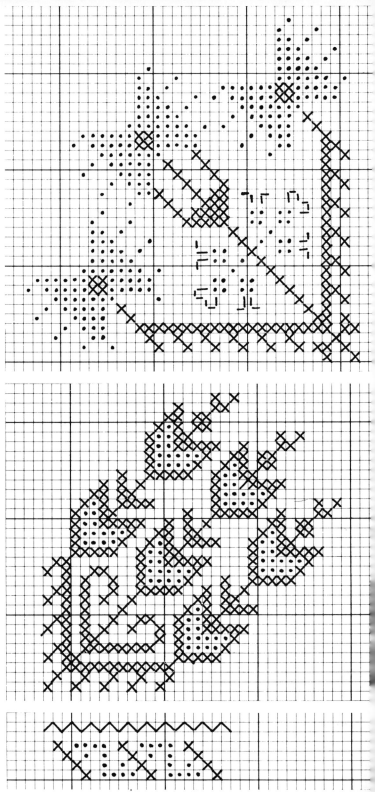

Blouse from Athens. Cross stitches on rayon have been worked through a silklike scrim and later removed, as with waste canvas. Courtesy Katherine Turlis.

Drawn fabric and drawn thread

Cross stitching and drawn fabric are two techniques often found in combination. Drawn fabric is also called pulled thread or pulled work and is fabric with open spaces created by the tension of stitches pulled enough to compress the woven fabric threads. The term is often confused with drawn thread, which is when warp and/or weft threads are actually removed to create the open areas. Both are usually done on even-weave fabric, although some other weaves can be used. It is important that the weave provides definite warp and weft threads to manipulate. The silk blouse shown has drawn-fabric areas, adding a lacy texture to the raised embroidery. It was bought in the Chinese department store in Hong Kong, an export of modern China.

The sampler of drawn-thread work is by Fritzi Oxley. Threads are snipped and carefully woven back into the surrounding fabric or, as here, used to create overcast edges. Decorative threads can be worked over or with the remaining threads in a number of ways. The front panel of the tunic by Joan Schulze is also drawn thread with various stitches, including needle weaving in the front center.

63

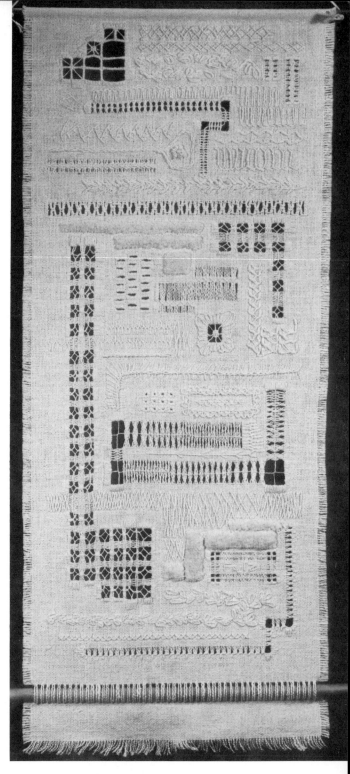

Drawn-thread sampler. By Fritzi Oxley.

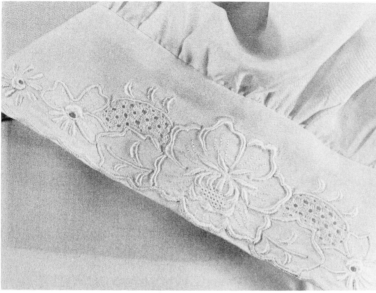

Silk blouse from China with padded white embroidery and drawn work. The simple floral shapes are adaptable to other techniques and treatments.

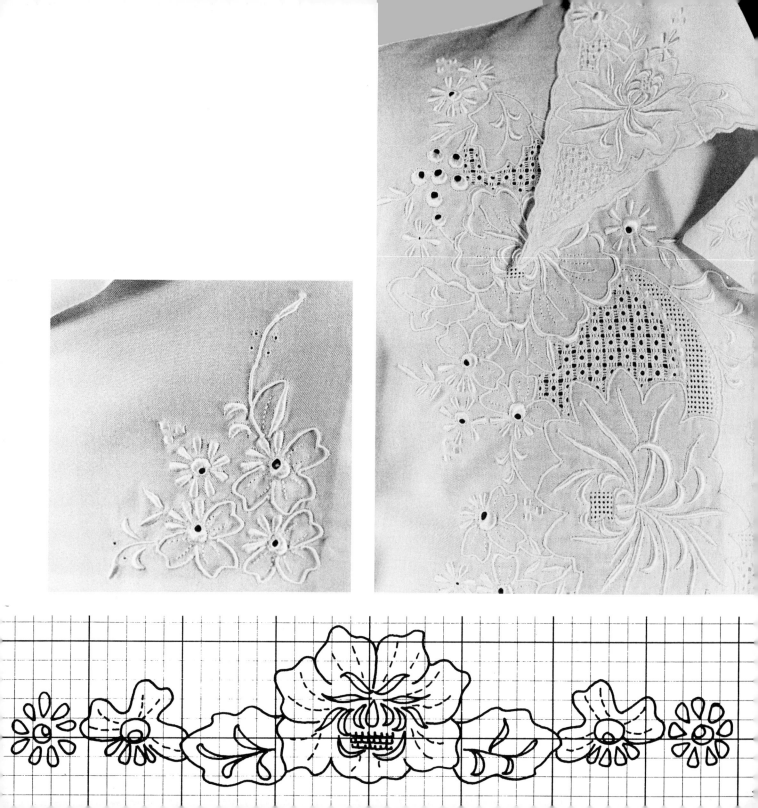

Blouse panel of drawn thread which started as a teaching sampler for Joan Schulze. Needle weaving and woven ribbons add color.

Reversible vest for night and day: satin ribbons, woven and appliquéd, reflect candlelight at night; and by day stitched embellishment and a drawn thread border add interest to an outfit. By Joan Schulze.

Drawn-thread sampler By Fritzi Oxley.

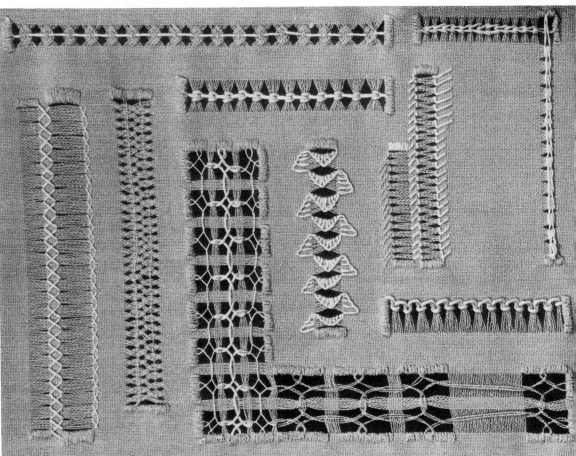

Cutwork

Traditional cutwork is done on a firm linen, worked along all the lines of the design. First, two parallel rows of a running stitch are worked. Then these are covered with a closed buttonhole stitch. After the embroidery is worked, the planned open areas are carefully cut away, leaving an open, lacy look. Several specific names are given this work, each designating a different amount of openness and laciness. *Mary Thomas's Embroidery Book* (Gramercy, 1936) lists: simple cutwork, in which the cut spaces are quite small; Renaissance work, with larger cut spaces, decorated and strengthened by buttonholed bars; Richelieu, in which added picots make the work still more elaborate; and Italian cutwork, worked around open squares and the most elaborate of all. Any of these methods can be padded for additional dimension and enrichment by adding rows of running or chain stitches between the initial two rows of stitching and working the buttonholing or satin stitches over them. When worked in this manner, the method is called raised cutwork or Venetian cutwork.

Cutwork has great possibilities with modern fabrics and styles. It can enhance collars, cuffs, yokes, blouse fronts, jacket edges, or skirt hems. The embroidery can be done all, or in part, by hand or machine. In order to retain the open effect, plan it for an area and a fabric that can remain unlined, and keep the back of your work neat, as it may occasionally be visible.

Choose fabrics according to their "hand" and their tendency not to ravel. Medium-weight, firm weaves, such as

67

Modern cutwork from Russia.

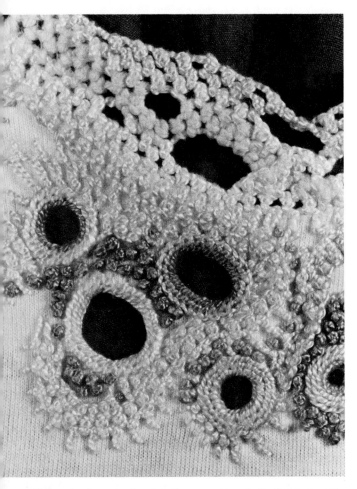

Holes, freely cut after bonding a cotton knit, finished with buttonhole and other stitches. Neck edge has been finished in needle lace. By Jill Nordfors.

cotton blends, wool flannel, and challis, all work well, as do machine knits of some firmness. Suedes (real or synthetic) can be used.

Fabrics too lightweight to work well as they are may be given enough body for cutwork in one of two ways. One way is to baste the fabric over a piece of tissue or other lightweight paper and work all of the embroidery by machine through both the fabric and paper. Tear the paper away after all the sewing has been done; then cut planned areas away. The second method is done with the help of today's bonding or iron-on materials. A fusible web can join your chosen fabric with a lining material selected to either match or contrast with the outside fabric. All embroidery steps are done through both layers. There are also bonding fabrics available, both woven and nonwoven, but they are usually white and likely to be stiffer than two lightweight fabrics which have been bonded together. It is possible to bond only the area in which the cutwork will appear if the inside appearance or difference in the stiffness of that area do not present visual problems. Test. If the entire garment piece is bonded, you might want to leave some area unbonded around seam lines. Then you can seam the outside fabric as you would usually and blind-stitch the lining closed over the seam, making a nice inside finish.

How much and which parts of your planned motif are to be cut away should be decided at the beginning. The amount and location of open areas affect both the appearance and the physical strength of your work. In simple cutwork, where only small areas are cut away, each part of the design is left firmly anchored. Larger cuts may leave sagging fabric unless you add bars or needle lace to keep it together.

If you are using a bonding method, follow product directions and bond the areas planned before you start any embroidery. Transfer your design to the right side of your fabric. Since all marking lines will be covered with stitches, you can use a permanent marker if you do so with care. Outline all areas to be cut with two parallel rows of running (if by hand) or straight (if by machine) stitching, approximately 1/8 inch apart. Work a closed buttonhole or satin stitch over both of these lines. Complete all other embroidery work in the total design; then carefully cut the planned sections away, using small, sharp scissors and taking care not to cut any threads.

There are several extra details you might want to plan for your work. Covering stitches can be given an extra dimension with padding. This can be achieved by running several rows of chain or running stitches—or a couched thread—between the two rows of stitches outlining the area and working over these with the covering stitches. Bars can easily be worked across the open spaces and can be worked as you go along. As you do the first row of outline stitching, stop when you come to a place where you want a bar to attach. Take your thread across to the other side, attaching through the fabric, then returning to continue on with your running stitch. Later, as you proceed with the buttonholing, when you reach the point where this thread is attached, again take your thread from your stitching line across to the opposite side, attaching as you go. But this time, come back across these three threads by buttonholing or needle-weaving over them. Once back to your departure point, leave no gap as you continue your covering stitch. When you cut this open space out, work carefully to avoid cutting this bar.

Jill Nordfors did a freely adapted version of contemporary cutwork on a cotton knit T-shirt (although any fabric could have been used). She first backed the design area with an iron-on fabric, but could have used a facing with a fusible web. Circular holes were cut out. (You might want to arrange cut paper circles to plan this step.) The raw edge of each circle is bound with the buttonhole stitch, worked so that the stitches are approximately 1/8 inch apart at the circle's edge. After completing the circle in the buttonhole thread, secure the thread, but do not cut off. Change to a tapestry needle and, using the radiating threads from the buttonhole stitches as the base, work detached stem stitches, as shown. You may change thread colors as you work outwards, or you may use other stitches that can be worked on laid threads for different effects.

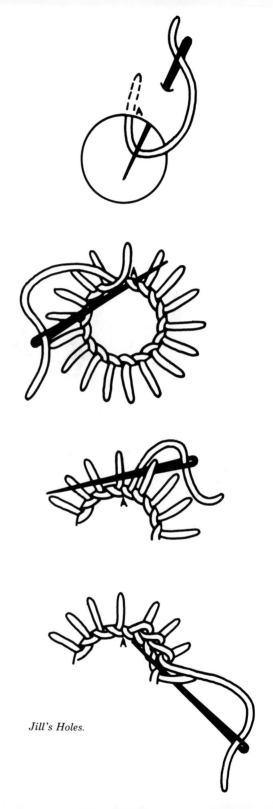

Jill's Holes.

Needle lace

The edging of the shirt is of freely worked needle lace. Essentially, needle lace consists of the detached buttonhole looped freely with a combination of threads and is a favorite of several artists. Jill, who wrote the book *Needle Lace and Needle Weaving* (Van Nostrand Reinhold, 1974), often uses it, as do Mary Ann Spawn and Helen Richards. Although the work of all three is dissimilar in character, this edging adapts well to each one.

Helen's caftan (see page 2) was made five years ago with handloomed fabric from India. When she found the Teneriffe wheels with the little silk tassels two years ago, she decided it was time to embellish the caftan. Planning around her twelve wheels, she worked primarily in needle-lace and needle-weaving techniques.

The needle lace works especially well for the washable knit velour that Mary Ann has used for several of her tops. Velour is bulky to face and, being stretchable, benefits from having a technique used on it that works with this stretch, rather than against it.

Bullion-knot flowers in pastel perle cotton and a broad edging of needle lace enrich a top of green velour. Detail of needle lace on red velour. Both by Mary Ann Spawn.

Neckline of red velour top with bullion-knot flowers and edging of freely made needle lace in various shades of red perle cotton. By Mary Ann Spawn.

Free embroidery

In an article about Mariska Karasz (*Flying Needle*, August 1978), Jacqueline Enthoven quoted this early pioneer of the free approach to stitchery as saying, "Stitches are so beautiful by themselves, they need not be pictorial representations. The very texture of the medium is rich and full. . . . an exciting piece of material serves as the melody for the interplay of threads—in, out, crissed, crossed, detached and superimposed—weaving patterns of new worlds and forming shapes that are different from yesterday, because today is a new day!"

This is the very heart of free embroidery, although experience has shown that even this freedom can be overused—that freedom without control and discipline lacks harmony. Anne Dyer and Constance Howard have both spoken of the sixties as the age of texture, when the fascination of textures that could be created by yarns overshadowed attention to good design and good technique. The best artists have now moved beyond any single dimension or any single technique and, today, are combining many fabric techniques—well planned to achieve a total design, a strong statement.

The free embroideries shown are successful for just these reasons. There has been little or no pattern drawing, no transfer methods, no imposed designs. But while they simply grew under the needle, every decision being made, and often changed, as the work progressed, sound principles can be seen at work here—unity, repetition, variety within that repetition, a limited palette with good value contrasts. The sleeves of Jacqueline's red dress (now made into a blouse for a new life) have a wide variety of flowers, but the repetition of circular shapes and a monochromatic color scheme (reds, light to dark, with touches of gold metallic) create the needed harmony. A dragonfly on one sleeve and the hummingbird on the other plus the placement of the em-

Semicircles of stitches worked around circles of shi sha. By Mary Ann Spawn.

71

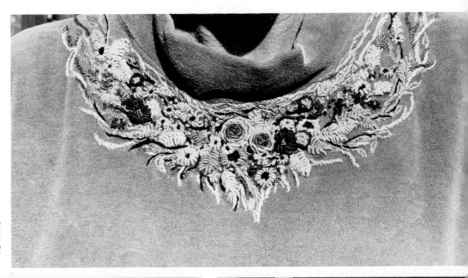

(Counterclockwise, starting at top)
Beige velour with flowers worked in bullion knots of beige, white, and blue perle cotton. Shoulder-to-shoulder flowers (detail on page 70). Entire shoulder of turqoise silk covered with mosaics of silk stitches. Clusters of bullion-knot flowers, bits of gold thread, and an occasional butterfly add interest. All by Mary Ann Spawn.

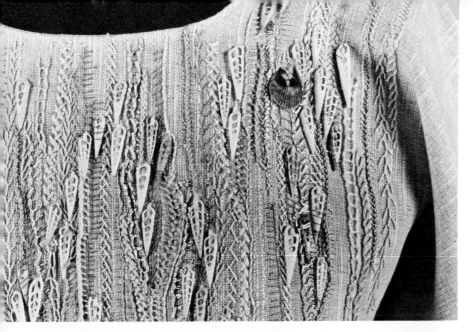

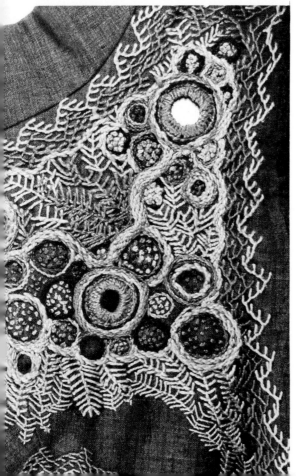

Detail of shell slices caught in cascades of stitches, the single scallop shell as a surprise. Various threads, all beiges, on handloomed cotton from India (full view, page 3). By Helen Richards.

Pattern of circles surrounded by fern stitches and bordered with triple-slanted feather stitches. Detail of the dress yoke seen on page 41. Dress yoke is cotton, dye-painted by hand, and embellished by stitches and shi sha. Both by Mary Ann Spawn.

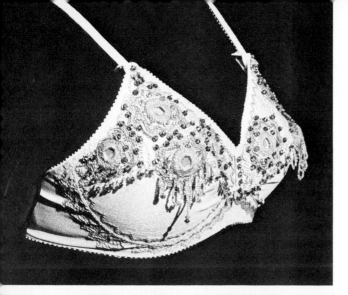

Stretch bra of gold metallic, embellished with stitchery. By Mary Ann Spawn.

Detail of bullion knots of perle cotton. By Mary Ann Spawn.

broidered area high on one, low on the other, are unexpected touches used to keep interest high.

The lushness of Mary Ann Spawn's work makes it a favorite of all who see it. She works completely spontaneously, guided by her painter's eye for color and texture. She works mostly in silk twists and perle cotton but is likely to pick up any thread that catches her eye. Her color collection of threads grew until her husband, Doug, finally helped get them organized on pegboards (similar to cribbage boards which he built to house spools) and in DMC display drawers bought from a wholesaler.

She has a marvelous sense of whimsy that often creeps into her work: a good example of this is the gold bra made as a gift for a particular friend. Another friend made the bra itself, out of metallic synthetic, and Mary Ann embellished it with stitches and beads of red and crystal.

But with all the spontaneity of her work, each thing is highly consistent in its thread, stitch, and shape choices. Her color palette is always highly controlled—with few colors, but good variation within those colors. The black-and-white photos show that her sense of color value is also strong. Many artists find their color harmony adequate, but sense a lack of punch. Often this is because, while the color contrast may be strong, the value contrast is not. Black-and-white photographs emphasize value contrast and are often used by professional artists in any medium to check for this contrast in their work.

Stem and feather stitches are favorites of Mary Ann, as is the bullion knot seen in photo. (She recommends using a milliner's needle to make the bullion knots easier.) While she uses other stitches, too, notice the variety she is able to achieve with just those three.

74

Special Fabrics

Embroidery is most often worked on solid-color, woven materials of various weights and textures. Each thread count, each fiber characteristic, each weave, and any kind of surface texture or treatment influences and affects the kind of stitchery that will work most effectively on it. Some fabrics take some special considerations.

PATTERNED FABRICS (PRINT OR WOVEN)

Using prints for appliqué is discussed earlier with appliqué techniques, but using them as a ground for embellishment is another possibility. The print design can simply be reinforced with stitches highlighting or outlining its motifs. Or the motif can be the starting point for shapes growing beyond the original shape, becoming something new in themselves. Perhaps because of their regularity, stripes can provide a good ground fabric. In the skirt by Ivy Jensen, the multipatterned stripes were offset very effectively by the

Multiprint stripe used as a background for meandering areas of needle lace by Ivy Jensen. Neckpiece is of crocheted colored telephone wire.

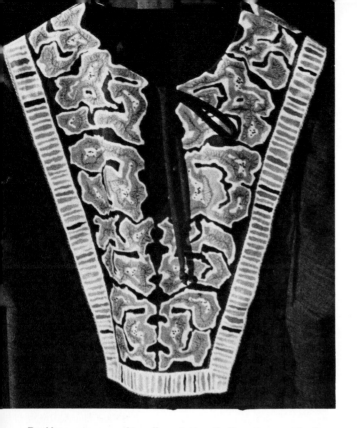

Real leaves were used in roller-printing the linen for a vest by Joan Schulze. Perle cotton, used in the bobbin, accents the machine quilting lines.

Inko-dyed and stitched yoke appliquéd to garment by Eleanor Van de Water. Design motifs were inspired by shapes of deer teeth, embellished with chain and Vandyke stitches and French knots.

Chain stitches in linen thread are worked on a handwoven, Guatemalan stripe. The surrounding seed stitches integrate the two patterns. By Melinda Phillips.

freeflowing lines of needle lace, which pick up the dominant colors of the skirt but hold their own strength by the power of their color and scale. Tiny stitches would have been lost against this strong pattern. The neckpiece is crocheted domes of brightly colored telephone wire.

The cotton stripe is in tones of blue, coral, gray, and white. Alternate white stripes on the yoke piece, front and back, were filled with randomly worked threaded fly stitch in a Danish cotton thread. Some of the spaces were then filled with closely worked buttonhole, repeating the blue and coral color of the stripe.

The handwoven Guatemalan stripe is part of the long coat by Melinda Phillips, shown in photo. She tried various thread and stitch combinations before feeling satisfied with the motif worked entirely in chain stitch and linen threads. The subtle powdering of seed stitches surrounding the motif made a smooth transition between pattern and stripe.

76

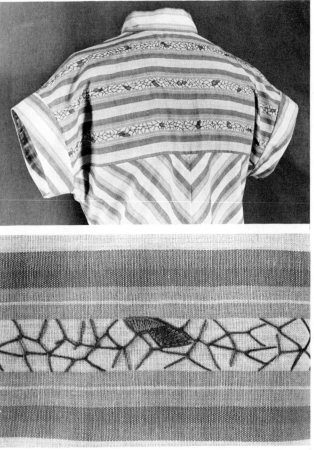

Cotton stripe, cut on the bias, used to create interest in dress lines. Leads to a yoke embellished with stitches of randomly worked threaded fly stitch in Danish cotton and highlighted by occasional spaces filled with closely worked buttonhole in colors of the stripe. By author.

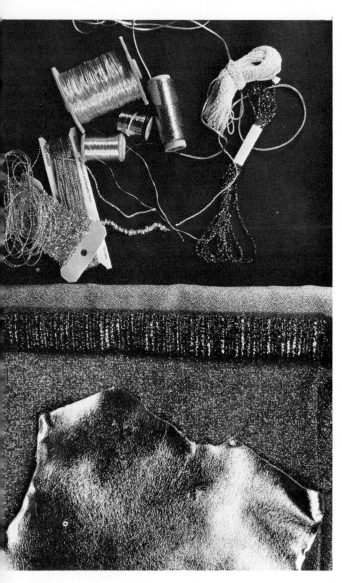

Various metallics found on the market—synthetics, except the gold kid at bottom of photo.

METALLICS

Have you noticed the proliferation of metallic synthetics appearing on the market these days? Not just in the metal tones of gold, silver, or copper, but in all the colors—pastel, primary, and shiny black or brown. Go into a yarn store and they have special threads "meant" (at least by the packager) to be used for needlepoint, crochet, or embroidery—fine threads that can go through the fabric for stitching by hand or machine, heavier threads and textures that can be used for couching.

The same thing is occurring in piece goods—all manner of metallics by the yard. They may be knit or woven in their construction and of all weights—from almost lingerie-sheer knits, to stiff brocades, to stiffer still, leatherlike synthetics. A fabric with any amount of metallic thread in it, whether a small amount of accent or the major fiber, must be treated as metallic.

Because these metallics are synthetics, they do not tarnish like real metal, they are lighter in physical weight, and are usually easy to clean. Keep an alert eye and an open mind toward new possibilities for them. New ones are still appearing and there has not been time for real exploration to take place, but the possibilities are there. I hope to hear from many of you who have good ideas that have worked for you.

Eleanor Van de Water used a gold metallic knit appliqué on a brown sheer knit over a white cotton upholstery fabric as part of a liturgical set. Machine embroidery adds texture, and the appliqué is edged by hand-couched metallic thread.

Other ideas to explore might be the quilting, including tra-

Synthetic metallics add richness to altar piece by Eleanor Van de Water.

Synthetic gold knit machine-appliquéd over a brown sheer knit over white upholstery fabric. By Eleanor Van de Water.

Pendants of embroidery on synthetic metallics. By Mary Ann Spawn.

Shadow embroidery of gold and silk threads on nylon chiffon.

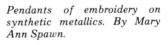

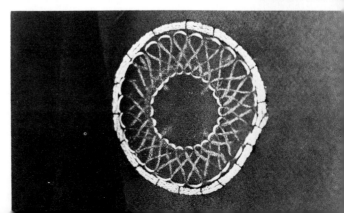

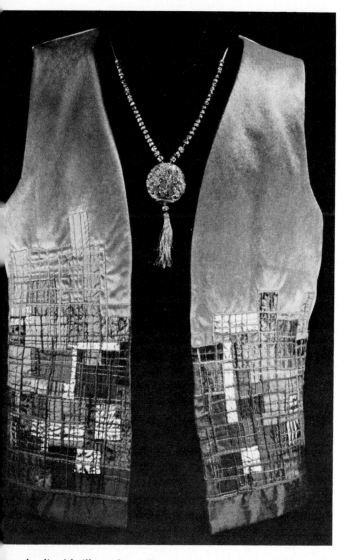

Appliquéd silks and metallics, with overlying grid of stitches on vest of brushed velvet (detail shown on page 8 and in color section.) By Mary Ann Spawn.

punto and Italian quilting, of soft metallic knits. The quilted area might be a collar, a set of cuffs, a midriff piece, or a bottom skirt band offsetting a garment of a different texture (perhaps velveteen or something with a soft, draping quality). Whole vests, jackets, or coats could be quilted. Metallic fabric might be used for appliqué or inset pieces meant to highlight the garment's embroidery.

Here are some general tips in working with metallic fabrics. Buy enough fabric to allow extra for testing; also, buy according to the "with nap" directions for cutting, as metallics will reflect light differently from different directions. Use an old pair of scissors to cut both the fabric and threads (some threads specify that they be torn, not cut), as cutting can dull your blades. Test whether pins or needles will leave marks. If so, do any basting or pinning in the seam allowance. Use sharp, fine needles and pins. Sewing-machine needles may need changing several times, due to the dulling action.

Test which design marking methods will show up and whether or not the marks can be removed or need to be covered. Know if the material will run, snag, or fray easily. Test for ironing problems. Even the pressure of a barely warm iron can break some metal threads, and their heat tolerance will vary. You may want or need to simply finger-press, using your thimble. To store, hang metallic yardage over a padded pants hanger—do not fold or crease. Under-lining is sometimes necessary to prevent breaking at any stress seams, and lining your garment will keep the often scratchy metallic away from your skin. For the same reason, most facings are best cut in a lining fabric.

Much of this information may be learned before buying by reading the hang tag or bolt end. Note fiber content and care instructions and consider how this will affect any materials you plan to combine it with.

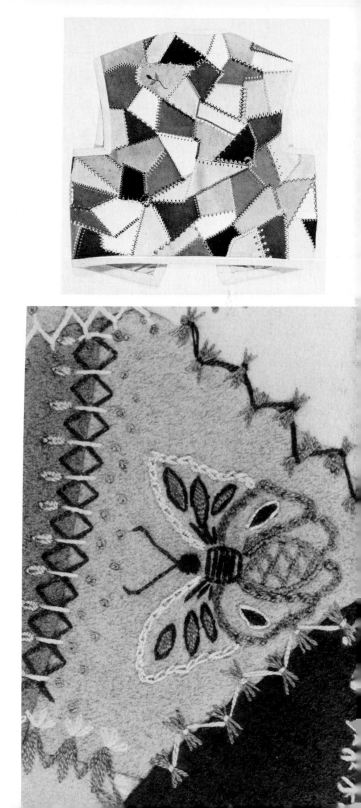

Back view of Ultrasuede vest (front shown on page 45). Detail shows stitches of silk twist on the Ultrasuede. By Louise Schwab.

OTHER FABRICS

Other special fabrics include velvets and piles of all kinds, satins, sheers (knit and woven), and brocades. Each has its own special needs, many of which can be ascertained by label information or in a good sewing book. Buying an extra amount of fabric for testing can save many costly mistakes.

Velvet, as a common term, has come to indicate any plush pile—from machine-washable velours, to decorator velvets, to fine silk velvet. Be sure you know the fiber content of the one you select. Plush fabrics should not be ironed with the pile side flat against a board. There are special "needle boards" available for pressing velvets, or a thick, folded turkish towel does well.

ULTRASUEDE

A new type of synthetic appeared on the market a few years ago called Ultrasuede, by Skinner. Introduced to the public through the designer Halston, it was the status seeker's dream-come-true, for several reasons. Expensive enough to be out of reach of mass production, it was still affordable to many people. And it was identifiable. But it soon became available in both ready-to-wear and yard goods, and a variety of look-alikes also appeared. Its increased availability has all but eliminated its snobbish element and left us with a solid addition to our fabric world.

As with any synthetic, there are people who find it uncomfortable to wear. And its rustliness, its somewhat stiff appearance, its feel, and its lack of give, are not to everyone's taste. Yet millions of others, men and women, have found it to be a luxurious, but extremely practical and versatile, addition to their wardrobes. It washes beautifully (all inner construction must also be kept washable for this; if not, the garment can be dry-cleaned) and needs little or no pressing. It is a marvelous traveler. It can be stuffed into the overhead

81

Canvas work, of similar but different patterns, inset as cuffs on sleeves of a pink Ultrasuede top. By Joan Bessom.

Canvas work inset as border of both vest and skirt of a rich, green Ultrasuede (detail on page 46). By Julia M. Goetsch.

compartment in an airplane. Packing creases shake out and it resists wrinkles and soil. And it can easily have a spot sponged out in a hotel sink.

People who sew have felt hesitant about tackling this new product. It is expensive, inhibiting the trial and error approach. And there are a few handling tricks to know about. But once these are learned, you will find that it is easier, not harder, to work with than conventional fabrics. There are several small books, usually available where Ultrasuede is sold, to help. One good one, by Pati Palmer and Susan Pletsch, is called *Sewing Skinner Ultrasuede Fabric*. It is self-published, but widely available.

These are general tips for working on Ultrasuede. It does have a nap, so always have it going in the same direction. It does not ease well, and deep darts do not lie smoothly; keep this in mind when looking for patterns. For instance, slightly gathered skirts will fit over the hips better than ones with darts. Seams can be overlapped and flat-felled, without turning, which takes slightly less fabric than conventional seaming, although seams can also be done in the conventional manner. Hems are usually put in with fusible webbing, which can also be used to hold seams open. (This is done by placing a narrow strip under each seam allowance.)

Patterns can be held on Ultrasuede with Scotch tape rather than pins. Pull the tape off in the nap direction. Pieces can be basted and pins can be used—the holes do not show or will close when steamed. Sew with 10 to 12 stitches per inch. Seams can be picked out and resewn, but repeated stitching can weaken the fabric.

As with any expensive fabric, you will want to make a muslin garment first or to use a pattern of something you have made before that fits. Ultrasuede has little ease so you will not want to fit it tightly. Inexpensive felt makes a good practice "muslin" because both fabrics have a tendency to hang away from the body, have little ease, and can be used without edge finishes, as they don't fray.

Many seem surprised that Ultrasuede has possibilities for embroidery, but ideas have hardly been tried. Joan Bessom and Julia Goetsch both used canvas work as an inset in

Ultrasuede—a good weight combination of fabrics. The Ultrasuede can be sewn with the edge flat against the canvas or sewn from the wrong side and turned with a conventional seam. While most would find it convenient to work the canvas first and then insert it, it could be worked after inserting if handling the shape presented no difficulties.

A patchwork vest by Louise Schwab is shown on page 45 and her procedures are explained. As Louise's vest shows, embroidery can be done directly on Ultrasuede. A thin, sharp needle easily punctures it with only a bit more drag than with many other fabrics. Many stitches, such as the stem stitch, need not go entirely through the fabric but can catch only part of the thickness, thus working up quickly. Vima Micheli covered her black vest with large flowers, using back stitch, satin stitch, bullion and French knots, and knotted and detached buttonhole. The bright colors and their textures are an excellent contrast to the smooth nap of the material.

As with felt or real suede, the edges of Ultrasuede do not ravel, making it possible to cut them and leave them with no further treatment except embellishment. This makes appliqué a natural, whether fully or partially attached. Examples are shown on the black dress with turquoise trim in the color section and the suit by Barbara Trellis on page 47, along with some of the details of the techniques used.

Another good potential use of this material is for cutwork. As in traditional cutwork, the motif should be stitched in before cutting. The cut areas will be stabilized by an edge stitching, but the stitches do not have to go over the edge to prevent the threads from raveling. Stitching does keep the edges from stretching along the cuts, helping your design to lie flat.

Ultrasuede presents some difficulties when you mark the design lines, because of the nap. This might be a good time to work with fusible webbing: tracing your pattern onto that, basting it onto the Ultrasuede, next working through the webbing right into the Ultrasuede, and then pulling or cutting the webbing away. Or you could machine stitch the design lines in place through the webbing, cut it away, and

Back view of black Ultrasuede vest enriched with flowers of needle lace. Front view and detail shown in color section. By Vima Micheli.

then work the design. Dressmakers carbon will mark, but will rub off easily. It can be gone over with watercolor lines, which last. The cutting of the areas to be removed is best done with an X-acto knife with a new blade that is good and sharp.

Because of its body, cutwork in Ultrasuede can be used in many more places than traditional cutwork: jacket or vest fronts, skirt hems, inset yokes or midriffs, belts. Since the pieces will not be lined and the back may well be visible at times, anchoring of all threads is best done under other stitches.

A variety of threads can be used with Ultrasuede. Since it is washable, you might want to keep to washable threads. Finer threads, such as floss cottons or silk, or number 8 perle cotton, are easier to use than heavier threads, but you can use heavy ones if you are willing to pull the bigger needles through the fabric. Couching and quilting can also be worked on Ultrasuede.

The very nature of fashion is change. Each new product offers new possibilities to discover and explore. As these new materials appear, it is important to look at each with an open and creative eye. Most of our techniques are ages old, but possibilities are always brand new. It's an exciting time and one when every stitcher can be a designer.

Blue-denim-jeans suit with appliqué of brown Ultrasuede cut in design shapes similar to those found in traditional Yugoslavian embroidery (detail on page 9). By Melinda Phillips.

Machine-stitched grape clusters and leaves on the magenta lining repeat the theme of Grape Cape by Eleanor Van de Water.

Finishing Touches

Just as a picture needs the right mat and frame to set it off, stitchery on a garment may benefit from a binding, edging, or closure to complete its total effect. The appearance of quality can be made or destroyed in these final details. Even the most beautiful work, if carelessly finished, looks less important.

Pay special attention to edge finishes and facings or linings. These are the areas where you are most likely to want to vary from a pattern company's suggestions. A good sewing book such as the *Reader's Digest Complete Guide to Sewing* (Reader's Digest Association, Inc., Pleasantville, N.Y., 1976) gives full instructions for a wealth of methods.

Rather than the usual turned-under facing, you might find that cording or a bound edge looks more finished around your stitchery. Or facing may be turned and stitched on the outside of the garment, instead of inside. You might want the facing to be of a contrasting color for emphasis, or of a firmer fabric to stabilize the garment shape. As with the stitchery worked on a yoke or an inset piece, stitchery might be done on a facing that is to be turned outward. In this case, if the garment is to be unlined, inside seam allowances may show at the finished neckline. Tack down the seam edges to prevent bulk or to keep raveling from showing.

You might plan a border of stitches around your design area, or you might want to use a binding as a finish. A binding is a strip of fabric stitched over the garment edge, one side of the binding on the garment's right side, the other

Chain stitches decoratively keep the lining edge flat in a knit coat by Carol Schimanski. Courtesy of Ferne Cone.

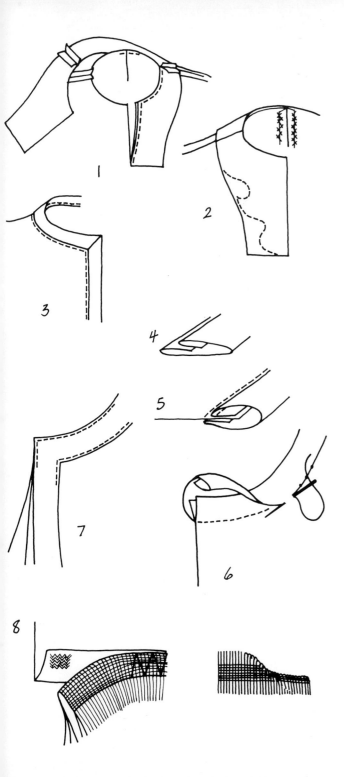

on the garment's wrong side. Bindings might be of the same material as the garment, of contrasting color or texture, or of a variety of commercial bindings available on the market. Bindings are easiest to attach smoothly if they are cut on the bias, but some materials can be manipulated enough to use on the straight if the curves are moderate. Leather or Ultrasuede can make handsome edgings whether cut in strips to be folded over the garment edge, or cut flat in the pattern shape, as in a facing. The amount of curvature needed and the weight of the leather or Ultrasuede will determine which way you do this.

Piping or cording also make nice finishes, and they too can be the same or contrasting fabric. Piping or cording is a folded strip inserted between two pieces of material when they are being stitched together. Then, as the hem or facing fabric is turned, the piping or cording becomes the finished edge. Piping is flat, with only the folded fabric as its thickness. To make cording, lay cable cord along a strip of material, preferably cut on the bias, then fold the fabric over the cording and stitch with the zipper foot. The size of the resulting cording will vary according to the cord. A tiny corded edge might finish the neckline of a delicate silk dress, while a long velvet skirt might have a dramatic width of cording around its hem.

Corded edges might lead you to other uses of tubing or lines as part of your design; try lines of Italian quilting or bias tubing blind-stitched into place. Tubing, like piping or

1, 2. Facing attached to the wrong side of a garment and turned right side out to be finished. Facing may be cut any shape (dotted lines). Raw seams exposed at the inside neck edge should be finished.

3, 4, 5, 6. Two ways of attaching folded bias binding. Fold and lightly press the binding as shown, making one side slightly wider than the other (5). The stitch-in-the-ditch method of attaching binding (3 and 4) is done completely on the machine. Lay the narrow side of the strip along the edge to be covered, right sides together. Stitch. Fold the tape over the edge and pin into place. Run a line of stitching on the right side, very close to the turned seam. Because the lower fold of the tape is wider, these stitches will catch the lower edge. The bias strip may also be blind stitched by hand (6).

7. Leather, real or synthetic, can be used for banding. If it is too stiff to turn, cut two pieces parallel to the garment edge to be joined as shown.

8. A narrow strip of woven cloth can be fringed and folded, then zigzag stitched over the narrow hem of a knit to create a fringed edge.

cording, is best cut from the bias but if the material is light-weight, tubing can sometimes be cut on the straight grain. Tubing consists of these strips, folded and stitched, usually about 1/4 inch from the fold, then turned right side out. For a rounder cording pull cable cord through the already turned tube. Another method is to use a length of cord double the desired length; fold and stitch the bias strip over one half of this cord, stiching with the zipper foot. Sew across the cord near the end of the bias strip and trim the seam allowances. When you pull the cord that is enclosed in the tube, you'll turn the tube right side out and will have enclosed the other half of the cord.

Spherical buttons can be covered with the detached buttonhole or other needle-lace stitches. Mary Ann Spawn covers various shapes of fishing corks in this manner for fastenings. Found drapery rings can be used in several ways to make buttons. One way is to work a closed buttonhole stitch entirely around the ring, then attach threads across the ring to set up the threads for weaving.

Inside seams are finished to prevent raveling or to provide a garment with high quality inside as well as outside. Seams establish the structural lines of a garment, and emphasizing those lines can often make a garment more distinctive.

Bias tubes can be used for simple loops for buttonholes or twisted into Oriental-type frogs or other decorative twists that extend at certain places to become button loops. A tube can also be knotted into Chinese ball buttons.

Make ties out of bias tubes, ribbon, or narrow strips of leather. Ropes for ties can be from perle cotton threads twisted together until they kink, then doubled back on themselves to let the twists come together. Perle cotton or yarn, crocheted in a simple chain stitch, makes good ties. Ties can be used for lacing through loops, rings, eyelets, or beads that have been attached to the garment.

Use your imagination for fastenings. Even an ordinary zipper put in by hand-picking will make you garment look more expensive than a zipper put in by machine. Hand-picking is a back stitch; short stitches with long spaces between them show on the right side of the fabric. One designer, when putting in zippers, changes thread color each time the color varies in the fabric itself.

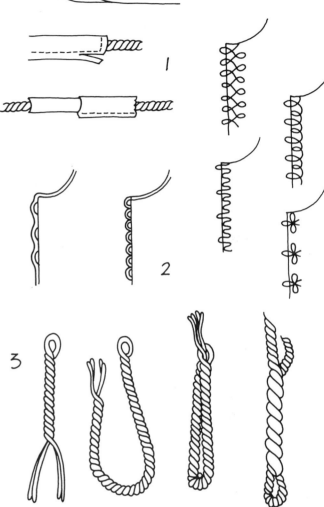

1. To make cording, take a piece of cable cord that is double what the finished length will be. Fold a bias strip over half of the cord and stitch close to, but without catching, the cord. Stitch across the cord at the end of the strip and trim the seam. Pull on the covered cord, pushing the tubing right side out and encasing the other end of the cord.

2. Braids, tapes, bias tubing, or lightweight cording can be attached in a number of decorative ways to make button loops.

3. To twist your own decorative cords, cut several strands of perle cotton or yarn, each strand five times the finished length wanted. Hold the strands together and fold them in half. Twist until they begin to kink. Fold in half again, looping around a knob or peg (try the thread holder of your sewing machine) to hold the cords taut. Thread the loose end through the loop at the opposite end. Release and smooth the twists. Knot or wrap near each end, then cut thread ends evenly for a tassel finish.

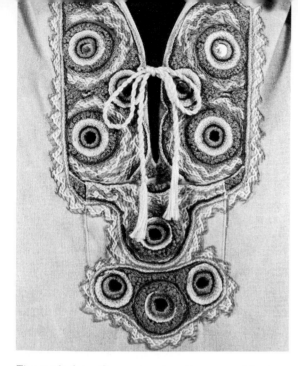

Ties made from the same perle cotton as used in the stitchery designs by Mary Ann Spawn.

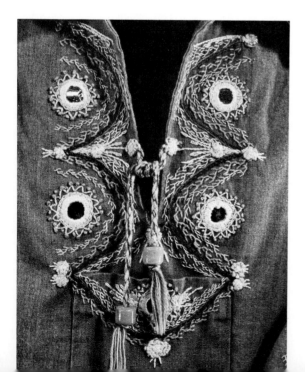

The correct button for a fabric is often hard to find, but there are many ways to come up with your own creation. Kits are easily found for covering buttons in your own fabric, lightweight leather, or Ultrasuede. Many shops will cover buttons. You might even want to add touches of embroidery to fabric for centering on covered buttons. The super-hold glues on the market today offer new possibilities for button-making. Small, flat buttons that have shanks can be glued as backing onto foreign coins, shells, or small polished stones. An active eye could make the list endless.

Several choices exist as ways of joining. A conventional seam results in a thin recessed line with no stitches showing on the right side. The flat felled seam has two parallel rows of stitching showing on the right side. Any number of decorative stitches could be worked over either of these seams with machine or hand stitches. Carol Sabiston covered the conventional seams of a black velveteen suit with a wide machined satin stitch that changed from one bright color to another every few inches, reminiscent of the colorful seams found in Mexico and Africa. Lines of feather or fern stitches can be effective running over the lines of the right dress.

Seams can also face the outside, as though the garment were being worn inside out. Then, as these seams are finished, they create decorative ridges over the garment. Decorative stitches can be used as holding stitches. Loosely-woven material can be joined flatly and attractively by a herringbone or Cretan stitch—but do a primary basting first. And, if worked in the same color tones, this stitching can set up beautiful lines of subtle emphasis.

Watch for ways in which you can add finishing touches that will complement, not distract from, your design plans. Leave your stitchery as the eye catcher, the highlight of your special style.

Glossary of Stitches

The following diagrams are quick references to the common basic stitches, to some personal favorites of mine, and to a few variations used in this book.

For further reference and more complete instructions, I recommend any of three books by Jacqueline Enthoven: *The Stitches of Creative Embroidery*, *Stitchery for Children* (Van Nostrand Reinhold), and *Stitches with Variations* (Sunset Designs). Since I've learned most of my stitches from her or her books, resemblances between these diagrams and her work is more than coincidental, and her kind permission is gratefully acknowledged.

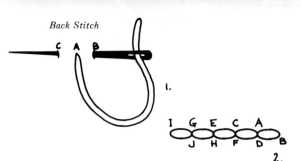

Back Stitch

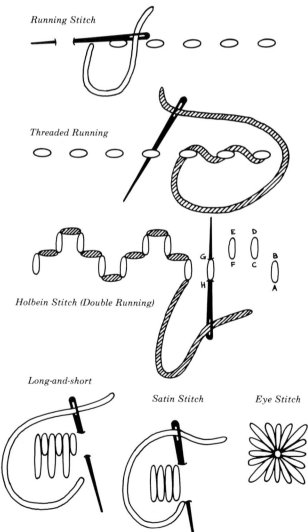

Running Stitch

Threaded Running

Holbein Stitch (Double Running)

Long-and-short

Satin Stitch

Eye Stitch

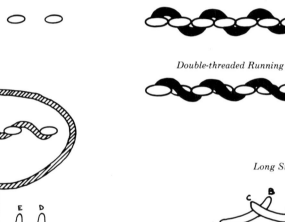

Threaded Back Stitch

Whipped Back Stitch

Double-threaded Running

Pekinese Stitch

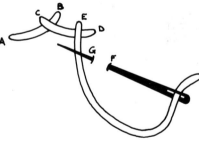

Long Stem Stitch

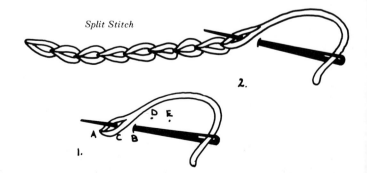

Split Stitch

Buttonhole Stitch

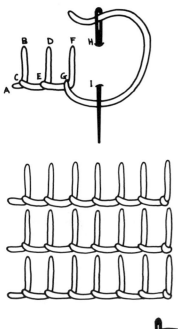

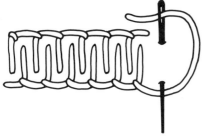

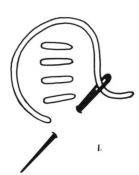

Up-and-down Buttonhole

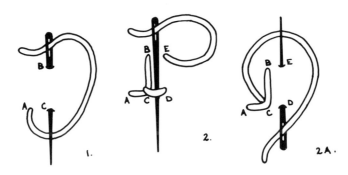

1.

2.

2A.

Chain Stitch

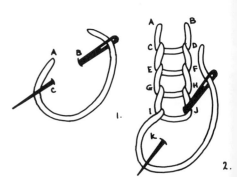

Up-and-down Buttonhole: Work the usual buttonhole stitch, ABC, as in fig. 1. The next step may be worked in one of two ways: for the method in fig. 2, insert the needle at D, bring out at E, and pull through. Next, slip the needle under CD, and you are in a position to repeat A. Method 2a is best worked on fabric of some firmness: insert the needle at D and bring out at E. Hold your thread above the stitch and under the point of the needle. When the needle is pulled through at this point, it firmly establishes both passes at the same time, and you are ready to continue to a new stitch A.

Square Chain Stitch

1.

2.

Raised Chain Band

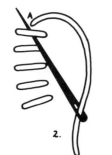

1.

2.

3.

4.

5.

Cross Stitch

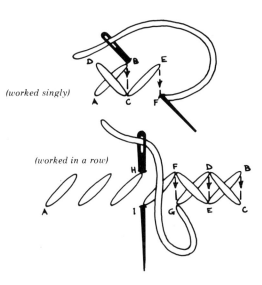

(worked singly)

(worked in a row)

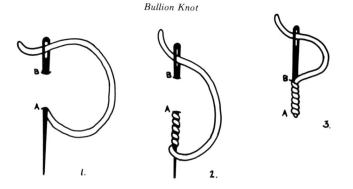

1.   *2.*   *3.*

Bullion Knot: Bring the needle out at A, insert at B, and bring out again at A, but do not pull it completely through. With the needle in this position, wrap the thread around the needle end for a distance approximately equal to the distance between A and B. Hold the wrapped thread under your thumb and pull the needle through. Insert it again at B, pulling the wrapped thread into place.

Chevron Stitch

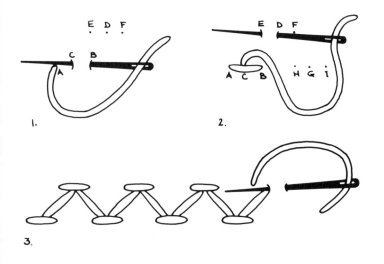

1.   *2.*

3.

Chevron: Work between two parallel lines, starting along the lower line ABC, as shown. Bring the needle out at A, in at B, out again at C. Move to the upper line and repeat, making DEF with the thread up, as in fig. 3. Bring the thread down for the next repeat.

Herringbone Stitch

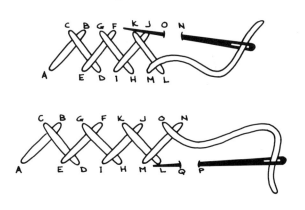

Double Herringbone

Cretan Stitch

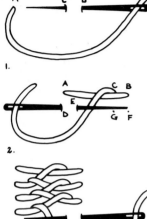

Cretan and Chain

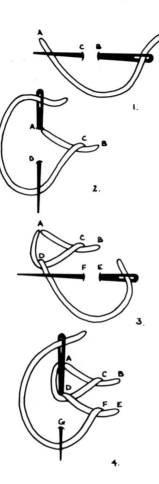

Spider-web Stitch

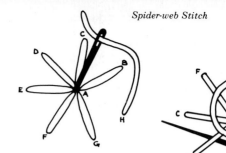

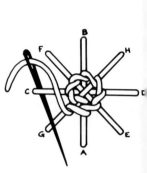

Spider Web: First, lay your foundation spokes. These may be laid from rim to rim, from rim to center, or from the outer rim to a small, concentric inner rim. If you are going to weave your threads, establish an uneven number of spokes, as in fig. 3. Once the foundation is laid, weave with a simple over-and-under motion of the thread, not going through the fabric. Or bring your thread under two spokes, up, and over one spoke with a back motion, then forward under two spokes again, as in fig. 2. Or bring your thread over two spokes and back under one spoke with a whipping motion as in fig. 1. Each method produces a different effect.

Threaded Fly Stitch

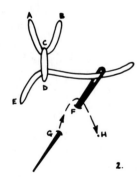

Threaded Fly Stitch: After working the usual fly stitch, ABCD, make additional passes by threading randomly through any of the "legs" being continually established.

Bokhara Stitch

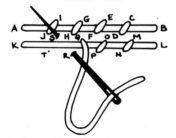

Bokhara Stitch: Lay a long foundation thread—A to B—and anchor it with the returning thread in slanted couching stitches.

Palestrina Knot

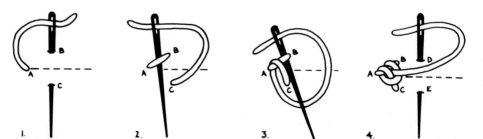